The *Theologian* Slave Trader

Christiana Oware Knudsen PhD

PNEUMA SPRINGS PUBLISHING UK

First Published in 2010 by:
Pneuma Springs Publishing

The Theologian Slave Trader Title
Copyright © 2010 Christiana Oware Knudsen
ISBN: 978-1-907728-00-6

Pneuma Springs Publishing
A Subsidiary of Pneuma Springs Ltd.
7 Groveherst Road, Dartford Kent, DA1 5JD.
E: admin@pneumasprings.co.uk
W: www.pneumasprings.co.uk

A catalogue record for this book is available from the British Library.

Published in the United Kingdom. All rights reserved under International Copyright Law. Contents and/or cover may not be reproduced in whole or in part without the express written consent of the publisher.

The *Theologian* Slave Trader

The Extraordinary Life of the Danish-Ghanaian
Fredericus Petri Svane Africanus (1710-1789)

*I dedicate this book to my children,
grandchildren and great-grandchildren.*

CONTENTS

ACKNOWLEDGEMENTS...8
PREFACE 9

PART I 11
CHAPTER 1: INTRODUCTION...12
CHAPTER 2: A BRIEF INTRODUCTION TO EUROPEAN SLAVE TRADING ON THE GUINEA COAST 16
CHAPTER 3: THE DANISH-NORWEGIAN KINGDOM AND THE AFRICAN SLAVE TRADE...19
CHAPTER 4: MY MOTHER'S FAMILY LEGEND CONNECTED TO CHRISTIANSBORG FORT..27
CHAPTER 5: THE SLAVE MARKET AT CHRISTIANSBORG FORT 33
CHAPTER 6: MY GRANDFATHER'S CONTACT WITH CHRISTIANSBORG FORT 37
CHAPTER 7: FREDERIK: THE CHILD SOLDIER..40
CHAPTER 8: FREDERIK ON THE HAABETS GALLEY TO DENMARK VIA THE WEST INDIES 45
CHAPTER 9: GODSON OF HIS MAJESTY, KING FREDERIK IV 47
CHAPTER 10: FREDERIK'S EDUCATION..49
CHAPTER 11: FREDERICUS THE PIETIST 51
CHAPTER 12: FREDERICUS THE MISSIONARY.......................................54
CHAPTER 13: TRINA IS SEDUCED 60
CHAPTER 14: FREDERICUS THE SLAVE TRADER...................................63
CHAPTER 15: THE ASANTE KING, NANA OPOKU WARE INVADES THE COAST.......66
CHAPTER 16: THE IMPRISONMENT OF FREDERICUS...........................69
CHAPTER 17: REUNION...73
CHAPTER 18: THE GENERAL DECLARATION..75
CHAPTER 19: THE PARISH CLERK AT HAVREBJERG VICARAGE 78
CHAPTER 20: THE TRAGIC END OF FREDERICUS 84

PART II 87

FREDERICUS AUTOBIOGRAPHY: THE GENERAL DECLARATION 88

INTRODUCTION 88

THE ORIGINAL MANUSCRIPT 89

[FREDERICUS WRITES ABOUT HIS LONELINESS AT UNIVERSITY] 90

[FREDERICUS FINDS REFUGE WITH THE PIETISTS] 93

[FREDERICUS DECIDES TO LEAVE DENMARK] 94

[FREDERICUS'S MARRIAGE AND JOURNEY TO THE GUINEA COAST] 96

[FREDERICUS AND WIFE ARRIVE ON THE GUINEA COAST, 3rd AUGUST, 1735] 98

[FREDERICUS EMBARRASSED AS PREGNANT CATHARINA CONTINUED TO WORK] 101

[FREDERICUS GIVES UP HIS DREAM OF MISSION WORK AND APPLIES FOR EMPLOYMENT AT CHRISTIANSBORG FORT] 102

[FREDERICUS WRITES ABOUT GOVERNOR SCHIELDERUP] 104

[FREDERICUS WRITES ABOUT GOVERNOR ENEVOLD NIELSEN BORIS] 106

[FREDERICUS WRITES ABOUT THE PASTOR IN CHARGE OF THE FORT] 108

[FREDERICUS WRITES ABOUT GOVERNOR PEDER JURGENSEN] 109

[FREDERICUS VISITS FREDENSBORG FORT] 112

[FREDERICUS'S DISTURBING MESSAGE ARRIVES FROM COPENHAGEN] ... 112

[FREDERICUS WRITES ABOUT PASTOR OLUF DORPH] 115

[FREDERICUS ATTEMPTS TO MAKE PEACE AMONGST THE OFFICIALS AT CHRISTIANSBORG] 116

[FREDERICUS PLANS TO BUILD A MANSION FOR HIS WIFE AND SON] 120

[FREDERICUS ORGANIZES A LAVISH PARTY WITH GOLD ORNAMENTS AS GIFTS] 120

[FREDERICUS GOES ON BOARD A FRENCH SLAVE SHIP TO SELL SLAVES] 125

[FREDERICUS STARTS HIS BUILDING PROJECT IN EARNEST] 126

[FREDERICUS IS ACCUSED OF BEING A TRAITOR] 130

[FREDERICUS'S FIRST ARREST NOVEMBER 1742] 135

[FREDERICUS IS ARRESTED AGAIN AND IMPRISONED] 140

[FREDERICUS DESCRIBES THE EFFECTS OF ALCOHOLIC DRINKS FROM CHRISTIANSBORG ON THE LOCAL VILLAGERS] 145

The *Theologian* Slave Trader

[FREDERICUS CONTINUES TO DESCRIBE HIS SECOND ARREST] 150

[FREDERICUS'S BELONGINGS ARE AUCTIONED AND THE FOUNDATION OF HIS BUILDING DESTROYED] 156

[FREDERICUS IS RELEASED AS GLOB DORPH IS SWORN IN AS THE NEW GOVERNOR] 160

[FREDERICUS WRITES ABOUT THE DISMISSAL OF GOVERNOR DORPH] 162

[FREDERICUS WRITES ABOUT JURGEN BILLSEN'S GOVERNORSHIP] 165

[FREDERICUS DESCRIBES THE REBELLION AT CHRISTIANSBORG FORTRESS] 166

[FREDERICUS WRITES ABOUT THE SHORT GOVERNORSHIP: "AD INTERIM EXTRAORDINAIRUS" OF SIMON KLEiN] 174

[FREDERICUS WRITES ABOUT GOVERNOR BILLSEN'S DEATH] 177

[FREDERICUS WRITES ABOUT GOVERNORS PLATFOD AND BROCH] 178

[FREDERICUS WRITES ABOUT GOVERNOR JOHANNES WILDERS] 182

[FREDERICUS WRITES ABOUT GOVERNOR AUGUST HACHENBERG] 183

[FREDERICUS WRITES ABOUT JOOST PLATFOD'S GOVERNORSHIP] 186

[FREDERICUS CONCLUDES] 190

POSTCRIPT 195

Selected Bibliography 196

About the Author 199

ACKNOWLEDGEMENTS

I would like to thank the director of the King's Library Archives, Copenhagen, Denmark, who, in 1988, allowed me to copy Frederik Petersen Svane's hand written autobiography from old Gothic script to be translated into Old Danish. He also kindly supplied me with the drawing of Christiansborg Fort by an unknown artist. I would like to thank Kirsten Nielsen, who translated this very difficult document from Old Danish into English. Thanks must go to illustrator, Rikke Kolkur Sørensen, who has produced the illustrations giving an impression of the dress of the period and to Coral Page for the artistic impression of my late grandfather. Thanks must also go to Dr Michael Welch, who proofread and offered criticism of the first draft of this manuscript. My thanks also go to Janet Lack Knudsen, a teacher and film producer, who put final touches to the manuscript. I would like to thank the lecturers at the Department of Anthropology, Aarhus University, Denmark, who, many years ago, encouraged me to write this book. Finally, many family members and friends have also helped with this project and I would like to say a big 'thank you' to you all.

PREFACE

MY INTEREST IN FREDERICUS' LIFE STORY

My interest in writing the story of Fredericus Petri Svane Africanus came about because, having lived in Denmark for over forty years, I felt I had many things in common with him. When I first visited Denmark in 1957 from Ghana, West Africa, with my Danish husband, Dr Peder K. Knudsen, I was shocked by two things: as a freshly qualified Basel Mission school teacher, who had been taught by her Swiss missionaries that all Christians, no matter their skin colour, culture, social status or ethnicity, were equal before God, I quickly found out, to my great disappointment, that this was not true in "Christian" Denmark. I found out that there were different types of Christian world-views amongst Danes. For example, some Danes I came across in the late 1950s, firmly believed that African Christians did not pray to the same European Jesus Christ and that European souls and African souls did not go and rest in the same heaven after death.

My next shock came on the day my husband and I visited Copenhagen, the beautiful capital city of Denmark. Beautiful well preserved historical buildings, a well-established parliamentary system, operating side by side with schools, colleges, hospitals, beautiful churches (some dating back to the 12th century). There were also bishops and their priests, and most importantly, the centuries old, University of Copenhagen with its knowledgeable professors. I wrote back home to my family, saying that how could a civilised country like Denmark, only one hundred and seven years before, buy and sell slaves from the Guinea coast? How could they treat the slaves as animals on the ships to St Thomas in the West Indies? As a young Christian woman, I wondered why some of the poor slaves were not sent to Denmark to work there and perhaps enjoy the civilisation later introduced to ordinary Danes? As time went on, I came to realise that the word 'civilisation', often used throughout history, does not necessarily mean that those societies who boast and call themselves 'civilised' live up to the claim.

Many years later, when I recovered from my shock, and when my husband and I with our three children came from Ghana to settle in Denmark, I went to study Anthropology at Aarhus University where I became interested in a story of one of the Mulatto figures at Christiansborg Fort, during the slave trade era on the Guinea coast. My interest in writing this biography of Fredericus Petri Svane Africanus is that the two of us have certain things in common. Fredericus´ mother, just like me, was born and brought up on the coast of Ghana. His father was a Dane; so was my husband. Fredericus was a Mulatto; so are my three children. Fredericus had a university education; so have all my children. All of us have lived large parts of our adult lives in Denmark. Finally, my interest in Fredericus' life story does not end here. As destiny would have it, both my mother's family and my father's family were involved, in different ways, with the Danish fort in Accra in the 17th and 19th centuries. So I feel that it is not just by coincidence that I became interested in the life story of this remarkable, Mulatto man.

PART I

CHAPTER 1
INTRODUCTION

Between 1451 and 1600, thousands of slaves, *black ivory*, were shipped from Africa to the Americas. They worked in gold and silver mines, on sugar cane plantations, even in the North American fur trade. In that part of modern Ghana - the Gold Coast - where the bulk of the slaves were drawn from, the European trading aggravated and triggered a series of upheavals and conflict between rival African kingdoms. Competition grew among these kingdoms for a greater share of the European goods, particularly, firearms and alcohol. These were traded in exchange for gold, ivory and in the end, of course, human beings. Eventually, the European traders laid more emphasis on the slaves, as a so-called, *chattel commodity*, than the gold.

The Portuguese, the Spanish, the French, the British, the Dutch, the Swedish and the Prussians were already operating on the Guinea coast when King Frederik III of the Danish-Norwegian Kingdom, in the early 1650s, introduced his state to this West African trade. Companies in Copenhagen received concessions from the government to trade on the Guinea coast. The most important of these Danish companies was to become *Det Vestindiske-Guineiske Kompagni* (henceforth: The West Indian-Guinean Company).

After the Danes had seized the Swedish trading posts on the Guinea Coast in 1657, Christiansborg Fort, was built at Osu, a village just outside Accra, now the capital of Ghana. This fort became the head office of all Danish-Norwegian slave-trading activities on the coast. Danish personnel in this outpost consisted of: merchants (købmænd), administrators, medical doctors, Lutheran pastors, soldiers, artisans and musicians. However, the establishment lacked Danish women. It was not only "climatic fevers" such as malaria, dysentery and worms, which had serious consequences on the health of the Danes. Excessive drunkenness, homesickness, involvement in prostitution, rape, crime and other problems, prompted the authorities in Copenhagen to allow the Danish men on the coast to marry African women.

The authorities also reasoned that such alliances would create stronger political ties with prominent African warlords. It would also help to produce loyal, Mulatto child soldiers and provide the fort with a supply of Mulatto girl prostitutes. Indeed, one Danish soldier from Christiansborg, named, Hendrik Petersen, married a sixteen year old local girl from the village of Teshi, another settlement not far from the fort. He gave the Danish name, Margrethe to his new bride. In 1710, they had a baby boy who they named Frederik Petersen. Unfortunately, his father died just a few years after Frederik was born, so that Margrethe's African family brought the boy up. At the age of just ten years old, Frederik ended up at the fort as a child soldier and later attended the fort-school for Mulatto children.

However, by a twist of luck, Frederik, the child soldier, was adopted by the newly arrived pastor at that time, named Pastor Elias Svane, so that the boy was renamed, Frederik Petersen Svane. In 1726, both of them left for Copenhagen. Frederik was baptised into the state Lutheran church, and His Majesty, King Frederik IV, no less, became Frederik´s godfather. Then the director of the Copenhagen-company which owned The West Indian-Guinean Company at Christiansborg Fort also pledged financial support for Frederik´s education up to university level in Denmark. Frederik had turned out to be a very lucky and exceptional young man.

While Frederik was studying theology at the University of Copenhagen, he adopted the Latin name Fredericus Petri Svane Africanus, as it was fashionable in those days for university students to do this when writing their names. Unfortunately, Fredericus Africanus was having a difficult time at the university and he joined the Christian Pietists movement in Copenhagen. This move aggravated his relationship with the Lutheran university authorities.

He also hurried to marry. With great difficulties he managed to flee back to the Guinea coast with his new Danish wife, Catharina Maria Badsch. On the coast, many disasters befell him. He was so poor that for the next ten years, he had to give up his Christian missionary project to go and work for the company at the fort. In addition to his administrative work, he bought and sold slaves to make ends meet and pay his mounting debts, as well as to finance his plans to build a large house in the village of Osu for his wife and son who, tragically, had been sent back to Denmark.

Due to the most extraordinary and unfortunate circumstances at the fort, Fredericus was arrested and charged as a traitor. He was put in iron chains and tortured and then imprisoned for six months in the "black hole" dungeon underneath Christiansborg. There he was fed only on bread and water.

Fredericus was released amid a revolt at the fort. He was then repatriated back to Denmark penniless. He showed great courage, an extraordinary sense of humour and a good command of Danish, Gothic and Latin languages in his writing when he wrote a plea with the title GENERAL DECLARATION in order to gain help for future employment. He sent this plea to the director of the company which financed his education, His Excellency Duke Carl A. von Plessen. In the plea, Fredericus gave an account of his life up to the ten years he spent at Christiansborg, and after he gave up his evangelical mission work at Osu. King Frederik V was informed about this plea, and later issued a decree that decided that, while Fredericus could not work as a pastor, he could work as a parish clerk.

One year after writing his plea, on the 1st of June 1748, Fredericus gained employment as a parish clerk and teacher at the village of Havrebjerg, south west of Copenhagen. However, one misfortune followed another. He had many troubles with Pastor Gunther, his senior, and many of the district parish council members. Aside from these problems, people in the villages around the area insulted him and made fun of him. He wanted to go back to Africa again, but he could not get financial help. Finally, Fredericus, as a toothless, deaf and blind beggar, died in 1789. He was treated as befitted a beggar:

no ceremony and his body hurriedly dumped in an unmarked grave at Slagelse Lutheran church cemetery, outside Copenhagen, without a gravestone.

A highly intelligent, strong and once handsome Mulatto, theology student, Fredericus was trapped between two cultures: two different worlds, at a tragic and un-Christian period in human history. He held on to his faith in God to the end. But he did not know where he belonged. He was never accepted in Denmark. However, as I will show next, in his ten-year autobiography, he unwittingly gave the world a rare insight into the daily lives of those who were engaged in the slave trading activities at Christiansborg Fortress.

CHAPTER 2
A BRIEF INTRODUCTION TO EUROPEAN SLAVE TRADING ON THE GUINEA COAST

The European trade on the Guinea Coast set in motion many changes in the socio-economic and socio-political systems of the Africans. Some existing, reasonably strong, kingdoms became more powerful, while others became weaker. With the introduction of European alcoholic drinks and weapons, and the subsequent great demand for slaves as *Chattel Commodities* by the Europeans, life for the Africans around the European settlements, as well as for those inland, changed. For example, the normal economic activities of these Africans, which had been hunting, fishing, farming, metal works and handicraft activities, as well as trading with the Arabs coming from the Sahara, changed. These Africans began to rely on African slaves for their European goods. The Portuguese became the first Europeans who supported, as well as guaranteed, the buying of these goods.

Christopher Columbus was a very young, sea-faring adventurer from Genoa, Italy, who had come to Portugal in the 15th century to find work. Portugal was seriously developing its agriculture in the Iberian Peninsular under the dynasty founded by the Grand Master of the Christian religious- military order of Avis, after the Muslims had left in 1249. But the order lacked Portuguese seamen as well as ocean going ships. Her ships were built in India, but workers and seamen were recruited from other European countries especially from Genoa and Milan in Italy. Earlier, there had been a lot of European slave trading within Europe. However, as time went on, a particular type of slavery, the *Commodity Slavery*, known as *Chattel Slavery*, where a slave was a possession, was abolished in Europe, leaving other types of slavery, such as temporary slavery to pay off debts, intact. Thus, the Europeans had to look elsewhere for *Chattel Slavery* and, therefore, turned to the African continent.

Hence, in 1441 the Portuguese captains, Antao Goncalves and Nuno Tristao sailed to Cabo Blanco, the modern Mauritania, on the West African coast, captured twelve Mauritanians as *Commodity Slaves* and brought them to Portugal. In 1442, the first shipload of slaves and gold from that part of West Africa landed in Portugal. In 1444, Lancrote de Freihis, a Portuguese tax collector from Lagos, formed a company to trade in Africa, so that on August 8th 1444, his ship landed 235 kidnapped and enslaved Africans in Lagos.

During this period, permission for Portuguese trading in gold, spices, leather and slaves had been granted by Pope Nicholas V, who issued Romanus Pontifex, a Papal Bull, granting the Portuguese perpetual monopoly in slave and gold trading with Africa. Thus, working for the Portuguese crown, Dom Henrique, also known as Prince Henry the Navigator, traded amongst other things, slaves from parts of West Africa from 1450. It was estimated that by 1451, thousands of slaves had been already shipped to Portugal. The Prince died in 1460 but the lucrative trade of shipping *Black Ivory* was still gathering momentum after his death.

During 1471, Columbus himself sailed along the West African coast and came ashore with his co-captain and sailors at a small village on the western shores of the Guinea coast. There, these strangers noticed that all the rivers from the interior entering the Atlantic Ocean were full of large gold nuggets. The chief of the village who came to the beach with his men, out of curiosity, to see these strange white human beings, was completely naked, but his locked hair was full of gold decorations. Columbus and his men quickly named the village "Al Mina" (the mine), now Elmina or Edina.

After the captains and their men had gathered as much gold as they could find at Al Mina, they went ahead and kidnapped as many of these *"jet black"* beings as possible and took them to their ship. They were not sure whether these beings were humans, and if they were humans, whether they had souls like European Christians. These Africans, of course, did not know where they were going. Eventually, they ended up in Portugal.

Thus, Columbus's initiative opened the door for Portuguese slave and gold trading on the Gold Coast, so that in 1482 the Portuguese brought about 200 soldiers from Portugal to build the first European trading fort, called St George's Castle. It was estimated that, at least a full cargo of 1000 men and women were stored in the dungeons of this castle at any one time. From this period onwards, many slave and gold commodity traders from the European kingdoms, such as the Dutch, the British, Spanish, French, Prussians, Swedes and Danish-Norwegians came to establish their own trading forts on the Guinea coast of the Atlantic Ocean.

In 1492, after his adventures on the Gold Coast, Columbus ended up in the Americas with financial support for a ship, equipment and sailors from the Spanish Kingdom, as well as moral support from the Catholic Church, who used this opportunity to spread Christianity to the New World. Many Europeans took the opportunity to migrate there, establishing new plantations and other businesses such as mining and fur production.

To begin with, these European immigrants used the native Americans as labourers on the sugar plantations, as well as in the gold and silver mines and on the beaver farms, but the hard physical work, coupled with infectious diseases such as syphilis, that these European immigrants brought with them, made the lives of the infected natives very short. They had no resistance to the sexually transmitted diseases and it was an economic disaster for the plantation owners. This made some Europeans reason that, from their experience, the African slaves who were brought to Portugal, even in captivity, by nature, were very hard working, tough and therefore able to withstand all kinds of hardships. Hence, the importation of these African slaves, to lay the foundations of the European economic boom in the New World.

Columbus himself finally returned to Spain where he lived and died a poor, lonely, unhappy and miserable man followed by a burial complicated by wrangles about in which country he was to be buried. But in appreciation of his contribution to slave trading which paved the way for a Spanish presence in the New World, and which also led to the opportunities for the Roman Catholic Church to spread Christianity amongst the disillusioned natives of the Americas, his statue was erected in Barcelona, by the enriched and grateful Spanish state.

CHAPTER 3
THE DANISH-NORWEGIAN KINGDOM AND THE AFRICAN SLAVE TRADE

By 1600, thousands of the slaves had already been shipped to the Americas from Africa's west coast. Consequently, on the Gold Coast, as well as from inland, from where the bulk of slaves were drawn, the European demand for more and more African slaves aggravated and triggered a series of upheavals and wars between rival, pagan, African kingdoms. Competition arose for shares of the European goods, particularly guns, gunpowder and alcohol, which were exchanged for gold, ivory and, of course, more slaves. A new kind of lucrative market had evolved at the Guinea Coast for Europeans. The Kingdom of Denmark was also to join in this trade in return for Danish goods.

The English, the Dutch, the Prussians and the French, challenged Spain and Portugal, with regard to their newly discovered trading territories on the Guinea Coast, as well as their sea route to China. King Christian IV of Denmark kept an eye on these developments. His Majesty naturally became interested in seeking out Denmark's share of the riches. He instructed his Councillors to set plans in motion for Denmark's trading in West Africa and in the West Indies. This was the inspiration for Jens Munk's expeditions towards the North-West Passage in the 1620s. However, King Christian's first plans, from 1625, in connection with this trading project on the Guinea Coast, did not materialise. It was not until after Denmark defeated Sweden in battle, that she was able to set foot on the Guinea Coast properly and to take over the defeated Swedish trading settlements.

Christiansborg Fort

Consequently, the Danish-Norwegian Kingdom took over the Swedish trading post at Osu, a village outside Accra, which had originally been a little trading post for the Portuguese from 1578 to 1645 and had subsequently been taken over by the Swedes in 1657. Thus the Swedes had owned two trading posts on the Guinea Coast; one at Cape Coast, on the west side of the Guinea Coast in 1652, and the other at Osu in 1657. These two trading posts were taken over by the Danish-Norwegian Kingdom in 1659. The latter involved many squabbles with the Swedes, the Dutch, the English and various local Warlords on the Coast, but in 1661 the Danes finally took charge over the Swedish trading post at Osu, and Christen Cornelisson laid the foundation for the bigger Danish-Norwegian Kingdom's trading post which became known as Christiansborg Fort, named after a Danish king.

The Danes then built other forts and trading posts along the eastern side of Christiansborg Fort. These were: Fredensborg Fort at Ningo in 1734; Prinzenstein Fort at Keta in 1784; Kongensteen at Ada in 1784 and Augustaborg at Teshi in 1787. But the Danish Guinea Coast trading headquarters, where most administrators, merchants, doctors, pastors, artisans, musicians and soldiers from Copenhagen were sent, was Christiansborg.

In 1672, a stronger foundation for this trading was laid, with such dignitaries as Niels Juel and his brother Jens Juel also involved. Thus, Danish goods were sent to the Guinea Coast which were gradually exchanged only for slaves. Sometimes one flask or bottle of an alcoholic drink was exchanged for one human being. These slaves were then sent to the Danish plantation islands in the West Indies, notably St Thomas. They would then be exchanged for sugar molasses that was sent to Copenhagen. These molasses were distilled into alcoholic drinks such as "Gammel Dansk" and "Akvavidt" and, together with "Dane-guns" and "Krudt" (gunpowder) would be sent back to the Guinea Coast. This Danish three-way trading became known as *"The Triangle Trading"*.

Danish African trading companies received concessions from His Majesty, King Christian V, to trade on the Guinea Coast. The most important of these companies, which was granted the sole right on the 20th of November 1674 to trade, was the West Indian-Guinean Company. It was established in Copenhagen, with well-known Danish dignitaries such as the Duke and Lord Chamberlain of the Royal Household, Carl Adolph von Plessen, and the Honourable Baron, Professor and Poet, Ludvic Holberg, who were among the richest landowners in Denmark, as shareholders. As Holberg wrote:

> *"The goods that are sent from Denmark to Guinea are chiefly aquavit, gun powder and flintlocks. The return for these goods, are gold, slaves and ivory, besides provisions for the slaves, for export. The company's ships load as many slaves as they can carry, and bring them to St Thomas in the West Indies."* (Holberg, 1921).

There were periods of time when The West Indian-Guinean Company suffered several trading setbacks and it had to be reconstructed. After one of the re-establishments of the Company, all the shareholders were hoping to make a huge profit on a particular venture. A ship called *Charlotta Amalia Regina Daniae*, named after the Danish Queen, was provided and was loaded with weapons and thousands of pots of Danish Schnapps for the Guinea Coast.

Unfortunately, the ship's crew experienced so many problems such as bad weather, sailors dying of tropical diseases, gluttony, alcoholism, and internal squabbles. This mission failed and shareholders lost their investment.

However, the company's directors made further efforts to find yet more shareholders and with the help of King Christian V, who ordered his officials to contribute 10% of their salaries to buy shares in this Company, they pushed ahead. Furthermore, the King ordered all rich Danish citizens who owned coaches to invest at least 60 Rigsdaler (old Danish Currency) to support the company. After the second reconstruction of the company, with the full support of the king, officials and the rich contributed to the creation of a solid foundation for the exchange of weapons and alcoholic drinks for slaves, gold and ivory on the Guinea Coast. Finally, the slave ship for St Thomas in 1673, *Cornelia,* arrived with around 103 slaves. The next ship, *Gyldenlove,* arrived on the island with so many slaves that it even surprised the shareholders.

The next ship in 1699 was *Christianus Quintus* loaded with 549 slaves from Christiansborg for St Thomas. In 1700, *Fredericus Quartus,* left the Fort with 542 slaves. In 1705, *Cron Printzen*, left Christiansborg Fort with 460 male slaves and 360 female slaves, all bound for St Thomas in the Danish West Indies. However, as cruel destiny would have it, the ship was involved in an accident off the coast of the Island of Principe in the West Indies, so that out of the 820 slaves, only five slaves survived. This terrible accident, however, did not deter the shareholders from continuing their lucrative business.

As the trading between The West Indian-Guinean Company and the coastal kingdoms along the Guinea coast gathered momentum, the Danish traders or merchants, the købmænd, started to change their ethics of trading rules by demanding slaves for their weapons and alcoholic drinks. After a while, when the tribal chiefs started to get addicted to the Danish schnapps, the Danes often demanded one strong man or a woman of a child-bearing age, or a teenager for a bottle or a flask of Danish schnapps. The rest of the slaves were then exchanged for weapons when the bottles of the alcoholic drinks for

The *Theologian* Slave Trader

sale were finished. But the Danes always had an abundance of bottles for their own use. It was estimated that sometimes a ship from Copenhagen would carry at least 40,000 pots of Danish schnapps, besides weapons such as "Daneguns" and gunpowder.

Eventually, the alcohol influenced the natives to fight more in order to capture more war prisoners as slaves which, in turn, provided them with more alcoholic drinks, a cruel and vicious circle. At Christiansborg Fort, the Danish Christian Lutheren Pastor in charge, held regular church services for God's protection and success for the traders. The Danish surgeon in charge at the fort also played his part by seeing to it that the Danes had good health in order to be successful in their transactions.

This was a very significant period in the Danish-African slave trade. First, the monarch in Denmark had absolute power. Aside from this, the slave trade was in the hands of a few merchants in Copenhagen. Second, because of the great economic difficulties that were facing Denmark at that time, the kingdom needed income from the taxes and share dividends from the slave trade and also from the Danish sugar plantations in the West Indies. As such, no court verdict whatsoever from Denmark prohibited the export of African slaves. Thirdly, many leading slave-merchants, who were also prominent figures in the Danish Enlightenment debate, and some of these enlightened slave merchants and plantation owners were supporting quite generously, poor poets and the agrarian reforms which were going on in Denmark at the time, so that some of the profits from the slave trading reached down to many ordinary Danes.

The prominent Bishop, Eric Pontoppidan, wrote a long preface for the slave-merchant Ludvig Ferdinand Romer´s book about slave trading on the Guinea Coast, published in 1760, in which he defended the African slave trade. He did his best to unite Pietism and the European Enlightenment movement. In 1735, he became Court Chaplain for King Christian VI, who showed sympathy for Pietism. After the King's death, in 1746, Eric Pontoppidan became the Bishop of Bergen in Norway and, in 1755, he occupied the Chair of Deputy Chancellor at the University of Copenhagen. Still defending the Negro Slavery from the theological viewpoint, claiming that slave trading on the Guinea Coast was a good mission of Christianity, he argued that "Christian freedom" which is freedom of the soul was separate from "physical freedom" and that the Africans were better off coming out of pagan Africa to the West Indies, and that Africans back home in West Africa did not need to hear the Word of God. The Moravian Brethren Missionaries bought their own plantation with slave labourers in the West Indies and 'proved' to the Danish public that Christian slaves worked harder than non-Christian slaves.

Eric Pontoppidan's attitude reflected the attitude of Pietism of the Danish-Norwegian monarchy, the Danish intellectual attitude to African slavery, as well as the Danish Christian's attitude. The Church in Denmark argued that even the New Testament and the early Christian Church accepted slavery as an integral part of the European social order and that, spiritually, master and slave were equal, but in this physical world, a slave had to accept his or her position as a bought servant. (See Corrinthians VII and Colossians III.)

Throughout the two hundred years that the Danes were on the Guinea Coast, Denmark did not establish itself as a sole major colonial power. It paid land taxes and, in addition, gave gifts to the local warlords along the Coast where Danish Forts and Trading Posts were established. Therefore, the Danes counted on the help of these warlords in the event of aggression from the other Europeans. These local warlords also saw to it that regular slaves from the various interior kingdoms reached the Danish Fort's safely. But this new way of making a living, gradually destroyed the local people's way of life, such as their traditional way of making a living from farming, fishing, hunting and metal works. They were not aware of the well-educated Christians' carefully calculated traps set with the dependency on alcohol on their coast. Consequently, these confused tribesmen were tricked into betraying their own brothers and sisters by buying European weapons for slaves.

Though the slave trading was gathering momentum at the Danish Forts of Christiansborg Fort at Osu, Augustaborg Fort at Teshi,

The *Theologian* Slave Trader

Fredensborg Fort at Store Ningo, Kongensteen Fort at Ada and Prindsens Fort at Keta, the establishment lacked Danish women. It was not only climatic fevers, such as malaria, dysentery, worms, but also other problems such as alcoholism, gluttony, criminality, fights, theft, rape, homesickness, lonely involvement in prostitution with the local village women, which had serious consequences on the health of the Danes in their settlements. These problems prompted the company management to allow employees of the company to marry local African women. The management also saw other important benefits of such intermarriages. First, it was reasoned that, besides giving the establishment female partners, such an alliance could create stronger political ties with the prominent local villagers. Second, such intermarriages would help produce loyal Mulatto child soldiers, Mulatto girl prostitutes and wives. Third, the alliance would also help further efficiency in the way that the local people could find means and methods of bringing more slaves to the Forts.

On the whole, the Danish slave-merchants, the good and civilised, the well educated, and the well to do in Denmark, firmly believed that the Africans had no souls, but believed that they were some kind of animal species. However, the great historian of Africa, Basil Davidson, condemned Pontoppidan's allegation that Africans were miserable in material terms, as the great distortion but claimed that Eric Pontoppidan was indeed the mouthpiece of the Danish society. Even though the Danes officially abolished their slave-trading activities on the Guinea Coast from 1803, and then had to leave later on, as their other business activities did not succeed, Pontoppidan's ideology lived on in Denmark, even up until 1917, when the Danes sold their last slaves on their West Indian Islands to America for cash, instead of giving the islanders independence. After the Danes had officially sold Christiansborg Fort to the British in 1850, for £10,000 pounds sterling, they left. A few private traders however continued for a while to sell Danish goods while others also tried to establish a plantation known as Frederiksgave, a few kilometres north of Christiansborg Fort, without success.

Some historians have estimated that, about 45 million slaves reached the New World, whereas about 90 million died during transportation across the Atlantic Ocean. Others calculate that one third of the whole African population was sold as slaves. In this connection, the following questions are being raised, by many people who are interested in the history of the African slavery period, concerning the fact that companies in the Danish-Norwegian kingdom were significant slave dealers during that era. How many slaves did they sell at markets at their Forts? How many did they ship themselves? How many of these slaves died at their hands in the Christiansborg Fort dungeons? How many slaves died during shipment? And, the last important question is: why is it that, none of these slaves were sent directly to the Danish-Norwegian Kingdom itself, to go and work in Danish fields, in order to be absorbed into the Danish Welfare system, as the Portuguese did with their slaves?

CHAPTER 4
MY MOTHER'S FAMILY LEGEND CONNECTED TO CHRISTIANSBORG FORT

I was born and brought up in the Gold Coast, at Kwaben, in the Kingdom of Akim Abuakwa, part of the Eastern Region of Ghana. However, my mother's Akan Aduana Clan family came from the Ashanti region, near Kumase, the capital town of the Central Region. My mother's family has told me the historical legend of Nana Yaa Pokuaa.

The legend goes that about five hundred years after the Akans had migrated first from the Eastern Sahara Desert near Egypt to the ancient Ghana Empire in the North African Savannah, they moved southwards towards the forested region of the Guinea Coast. A large group of these Akan Clans' immigrants settled down in the region now known as the Ashanti Region of Ghana.

These immigrants then divided into twelve clans and started to organise themselves to develop the surrounding country. Apart from occasional minor conflicts with other neighbouring kingdoms, they tried to busy themselves with building their settlements. Their economic activities were varied: they hunted for both game and ivory, they cultivated the land for foodstuffs, they made their clothes from weaving and also from the bark of certain trees, they made their sandals from wood, they washed gold for their ornaments, they worked all sorts of metals, they carved wood and made pottery. These goods were traded with the Arabs and Berbers from the Sahara Desert. Besides their economic activities, and as well as being great warriors, the clans set up their own constitution, laws, moral code and customs.

All these economic and political activities were interwoven with their religion based on the Almighty God, the Creator, "Onyankopon", whom they worshipped through ancestral spirits and lesser gods. All medicine men and women (Witch-doctors) relied on the will of this creator for success.

One of the clan groups within this emerging Ashanti Kingdom was my mother's royal, Aduana Clan, of Asantemanso, outside Asumagya, an important division of the Kingdom. As my mother's family oral legend goes, a young royal woman from their family was married to a local Asona clan's powerful warlord. This young woman ruled as Queen Mother, side by side with her uncle, her mother's brother, the divisional chief. In Akan matrilineal cultural heritage, queens were mothers or mothers' sisters, or sisters of kings and chiefs.

One day a petty incident in a neighbouring kingdom triggered a chain of unforeseen events within two of the neighbouring kingdoms that turned out to be catastrophic for my mother's family. As the legend goes, the son of a powerful neighbouring king was sent to lead a delegation to a rival kingdom to collect a tribute. It was alleged that this young man tried to seduce a pretty royal woman from the rival kingdom who was at the riverside to bathe with her friends. When the king of the rival kingdom heard about this, he refused to pay the taxes and also ordered this young man's untouchable beard to be shaven off as punishment.

This was taboo for the young man and his family so this incident triggered a war between those two kingdoms which, in turn, led to instability and upheavals among many of the small kingdoms in that whole area. Events got to a stage where, because of matrilineal inheritance, this young Queen Mother, Nana Yaa Pokuaa, and her two young children had to be protected, even though she and her people were not directly involved in the dispute. Therefore, they were sent into hiding while the various battles raged on in that area between those two neighbouring kingdoms.

While the battles were being fought out, a local gold trader from one of the kingdoms returned from the coast and brought samples of three new and strange commodities to show to his king. These were:

guns, gunpowder and schnapps from the Danish Christiansborg Fort. Immediately, a delegation from this kingdom was despatched carrying with them a large quantity of gold with the purpose of selling this gold in order to purchase the new weapons for their war. However, after many days and nights of walking, they reached Christiansborg Fort but by then the Danes had just discovered a form of payment much valuable than gold for their goods. They demanded human beings as the only acceptable form of payment.

The delegation returned home with their gold and without Danish weapons. At this point, this warring kingdom, out of desperation, decided to get rid of some of their war prisoners who, under normal circumstances, would have been absorbed into the clans of their captors. At one time, for example, in their history, war prisoners became so integrated and absorbed into their new captors' clan families, that outsiders would not know who were war prisoner-slaves and who were not, especially if these war prisoners did not have special tribal markings or did not speak the host language with accents. Normally, the male-slaves would eat and work together with their masters, the women would eat together, and the children of slaves would also eat together with the children of their masters. But when it came to the choosing of special royal candidates for special offices, those slaves were of course excluded. Nevertheless, there were examples where prisoners of wars who became slaves were allowed to establish their own villages, as long as they paid their yearly tribute to their new masters.

A group of war prisoners were quickly bound and made ready to be marched to the coast to Christiansborg Fort: men, women, children, the old and young. But as destiny would have it, Nana Yaa Pokuaa, who had been sent into hiding with her three year old daughter and eight month old baby girl, became caught up in the trade. Unfortunately, she was captured by mistake, together with two of her male entourage, by the unscrupulous traders who did not investigate the queen's identity. Neither did these traders speak the same Akan dialect, nor were they prepared to observe common rules in connection with royal war prisoners. Tragically, the three year old daughter was separated from her mother during the commotion and disappeared.

Nana Yaa Pokuaa, her baby, the two male members of her royal family and a number of war prisoners were bound. The slaves' right arms were fixed with iron-clamps attached to large pieces of wooden collars, which they could lift and carry on their heads so that they could not run away. Some of the women captured were bound together with strings of woven oil palm tree leaves. Thus bound, day and night, Nana Yaa Pokuaa and the other slaves had to endure a treacherous march through the forest, over hills, across planes, balancing these heavy pieces of wood on their heads or shoulders in stormy, tropical temperatures.

The very young children had to walk alongside the grown-ups also carrying small amounts of food. Babies were tied to their mothers' chests, and those escorting them carried whipping sticks, in case somebody tried to break loose or could not walk fast enough. Some died on the way from various diseases such as: malaria, yellow fever, dysentery, typhoid, as well as from snake and scorpion bites, or hunger or from attacks by wild animals. The exhausted slaves, who could not go on, were left at the sides of the paths to die and to be eaten by scavengers. The legend continues that Nana Yaa Pokuaa, her baby and other slaves were on this treacherous journey for days and days. These people, who had never seen either the sea or a white man before, were on their way to be sold at the Danish slave market.

On the whole, the cruel treatment that these slaves underwent during their march across the forests towards Christiansborg Fort was absolutely nothing compared to the treatment Nana Yaa Pokuaa and her fellow slaves underwent once they were thrown into the dungeons under the Fort before they were sold.

On arrival at the Fort, the Danes expressed satisfaction so the desperate traders were able to buy their weapons and alcoholic drinks. Next, the slaves were put into the hands of the Danish soldiers who escorted them into the dungeon. The dungeon was deep down under the fort, with no windows, no fresh air. Hundreds of slaves had to share this little space: men, women, boys, girls, children, babies and old people, as well as the sick, the dying and the hysterical. They were given very little food and very little water.

The *Theologian* Slave Trader

Marching to Christiansborg Slave market

On the next morning, the legend explains, when the door was opened by the Danish soldiers, the stench that came out made the soldiers sick as it hung over the entire Fort. The reason for the stench was that some of the slaves had suffocated and died in the heat, some had vomited or urinated while some had defecated. Some of the slaves then tried to help their fellow captives by biting their noses, or ears or lips, in a last desperate effort to make each other unfit for sale at the market.

Then the Danish medical doctor in charge of the health of the slaves helped the soldiers to choose those who were fit to be sold that day. The Fort's slave servants then cleaned them by pouring water on them, removing all hair from their bodies and smearing their naked bodies, both men and women, young and old, with palm oil so that the other European buyers could not tell who was old and who was young.

Nana Yaa Pokuaa was amongst those to be sold that day, with her baby hanging on to her empty breasts. After the sales, the Danish Lutheran Church Pastor in charge of the Fort blessed the transaction - but not the souls of the slaves - as the European Christians believed that Africans had no souls for Jesus' blessings. The soldiers made sure that the chosen slaves behaved well during the sales and, those slaves who resisted the demand for good manners, were whipped mercilessly. The slaves to be sold were finally put in heavy iron chains and assembled under the hot sun around a big tree in the courtyard of Christiansborg Fort.

CHAPTER 5
THE SLAVE MARKET AT CHRISTIANSBORG FORT

All was set for business at the Christiansborg Fort slave market. Foreign buyers came, notably the Danish traders, købmænd, the British, the French, the Dutch, the Spanish, the Prussians, anchored their ships off the shores of Christiansborg Fort, and arrived in small rowing boats to do their business. These traders then inspected the 'goods' and bought what they wanted. Those slaves, who looked younger, despite the oil on all of them, fetched the higher prices, especially mature young men and young women of childbearing age.

At the Slave market

The next step was the work of the buyers' smiths, whose duty it was to mark the newly purchased goods with their trader's logos and brand. The smiths put the iron brands into hot fire then removed the glowing hot iron from the fire and pressed it firmly on the chest areas of the slaves, who had been smeared with extra palm oil, in order to mark their goods clearly. As the female slaves used to develop serious sores on their breasts, these markings were done on their upper backs instead.

Thus, the legend of Nana Yaa Pokuaa continues, the morning when the young queen was sold, her buyer's logo was marked on her back causing a painful wound. The next step was that the Danish købmænd, whose purchases included this young royal woman, instructed the Danish soldiers in charge to send these slaves to the beach without delay. Next came the tall strong local village fishermen who were hired to transport the slaves on their rowing boats to the anchored Danish company's trading ship.

Departure from Christiansborg Fortress

The *Theologian* Slave Trader

At last it was the turn of Nana Yaa Pokuaa, who once used to bathe sitting on a solid gold stool and then sat on another gold stool on special ceremonial days, with her body decorated with pure gold dust mixed with palm oil, dressed in beautiful hand woven cloth with gold ornaments, to greet her clan members. On the day of her sale, she had to endure heavy iron chains on her feet and painful sore back, with her "paper thin" baby, hanging desperately onto one of her shrunken and empty breasts. The waiting rowing boat transported her to the Danish slave ship *Christianus Quintus* anchored on the ocean a few hundred metres from the beach. The *Quintus* was bound for the Danish sugar plantation island of St Thomas.

The legend tells that as Nana Yaa Pokuaa was being pushed onto the rowing boat by one of the Fort's soldiers, another crewman grabbed her baby and threw the child onto the beach a short distance away. Everyone on the boat could see hungry hyenas, which had been pacing impatiently backwards and forwards, rushing to grab the helpless screaming child. It was common practice for babies and children to be snatched from their mothers, on the way to the rowing boats, and be thrown to the hyenas by the soldiers. It was done in order to make life on the ships easier for the Captains. (Hansen, 1987)

Slave babies for hyenas

That day, sometime in 1699, the young queen mother, with the Danish slave mark **CB** on her back, was locked up in the hold of the Danish Slave ship. She could hear, in her mind, the pouring of libation accompanied by 'talking drums' at her funeral at Asantemanso outside Asumagya chanting:

Toppled Gold Stool, Nana Yaa Pokuaa, we sympathise with you.

My mother's family legend claims that, the three year old daughter of the queen, who was lost days before, was later found safe and well. She was my great, great grand mother. Later on, owing to internal family quarrels, some of these family members, including my great grandmother left Asumagya area to settle in Asante Akyem Yuoso, another part of the Asante region, where they continued their role as tribal chiefs.

Later, during one of the wars in the second half of the 19th century between the Ashanti and the British some of the royal females, including my grandmother, were again sent into hiding at Tumfa in the Akim Abuakwa district in the Eastern Region of the Gold coast.

Unfortunately, the head of the family, Nana Anti Gyan, the divisional chief of Yuoso and Amantra region of Ashanti, and a warlord of the Ashanti battalion, who was left behind at Yuoso, confronted the British army with his battalion in an effort to stop them from entering the Asante Kingdom. However, Nana Anti Gyan, was captured and beheaded by the British army on the banks of River Pra. This defeat meant that the Ashanti region became part of the British Colony of the Gold Coast, when the British formally purchased the ageing Christiansborg Fort.

CHAPTER 6
MY GRANDFATHER'S CONTACT WITH CHRISTIANSBORG FORT

My father's father, Nana Kwaku Ware (Oware), was a powerful "Gyasehene", a divisional chief of the Kingdom of Akim Abuakwa. Before he became a chief in the 1840s, as a young trader he employed many family members, as well as family servants, to carry gold across the Atiwa Range of mountains in the eastern region to the coast to be sold at Christiansborg Fort. Consequently, my grandfather came into contact with the Danes just before 1850 and just as they were abandoning their slave trading activities. He managed to sell his gold to the fort in return for goods and schnapps. It made him a rich man before he ultimately became the divisional chief.

When the Fort was officially sold to the British in 1850, my grandfather continued to trade with the few Købmænd traders who remained to do business. Unlike my mother's tragic family experience with the Danes, he maintained a good relationship with the European owners. In appreciation of this good business relationship, first he married a local Akwapim girl, my grandmother; second he gave Danish names to his three sons as their first names. The first son, my father, was named Rickard, later called Richard by the British: the second son was named Hansen; and the third son was named Johann and later called John by the British. The Danes also called Nana Kwaku Ware, Johann, but the British called him John. Nana Kwaku Ware then sent his sons to the local school at Osu village, which was established in the late 19th century with the help of some Danish missionaries.

However, paradoxically, my father who was the first son of my grandfather, Nana Kwaku Ware, married my mother, whose ancestor was the three year old daughter of the Queen Mother, Nana Yaa Pokuaa, who was left behind in the confusion of the slave march and later found by the family at Asantemanso outside Asumagya. Unfortunately, the Danish influence on my grandfather also had its negative side. It was known to the British that he loved Danish schnapps so much so that he was drunk on many occasions when he attended meetings with the British authorities. Also, when drunk, he used to embarrass local people by revealing the origins of their family trees; especially those people who came from families of war captives. This drunkenness was not confined to Nana. Some of the other chiefs in the kingdom also drank too much. Apparently, later in 1910, the British made "Gyasehene" John (Johann) Nana Kwaku Ware, by then an old man, and some of the other Akyem Abuakwa chiefs, sign an agreement not to come to meetings drunk!

Nana Kwaku Ware (Oware)

But Nana Kwaku Ware was intelligent and very witty. It was well known that his conversations with the British colonial representatives were full of sarcasm. However, he was known by his people to be an excellent ruler. For example, he would confront young men who were hanging about beneath shady trees in the villages drinking palm wine and give them machetes and instruct them to go out to the forest to cultivate crops. In the end, the divisional chief of the Kingdom of Akyem Abuakwa, "Gyasehene" Nana Kwaku Ware (Oware) (John), died at the age of nearly one hundred years old, and his wife, my grandmother, an Akwapim girl who had worked as a housemaid for one of the last Danish slave-traders who remained on the Coast after 1850, died at the age of 105.

CHAPTER 7
FREDERIK: THE CHILD SOLDIER

The Danish slave trading period at Christiansborg Fort from 1661 to 1850 was, and will always be, a dark and tragic period in Danish history. The interpretation of Christianity, and its practice in civilised Denmark at that time, failed Africans. The Danes took advantage of natives who were alleged to be people without souls. But the worst part of this tragedy was how the traders themselves became completely debauched at Christiansborg, despite coming from the upper reaches of Danish society.

The conditions of the slaves at Christiansborg were, from the 17th century when the Danes began their trading, beyond description. Not only were the slaves existing in overcrowded, inhumane conditions in the dungeons underneath the fort, the lifestyle going on upstairs was also dangerous.

The Danes suffered from "Climatic Fever". This term covered a bundle of diseases that afflicted the Europeans. For example, they suffered from: malaria fever, tapeworms, threadworms and roundworms, dysentery and typhoid fever. They also endured: alcoholism, rape, theft, violence, criminal activities, prostitution and homesickness. The result was that most of the Danes who were sent from Copenhagen to the Guinea Coast died within one year or so of arrival. There was a constant flow of new Danes arriving to replace the dead. The one mercy for the terminally ill was that, due to poor medical knowledge and conditions, they died very quickly.

Those who survived for a year or more had the opportunity to remain on the coast and conduct business. Unfortunately, even after this period, there was still the danger of dying on the ship on the way back home to Denmark. The ships had to sail to the West Indies to unload the slaves first and then load molasses for the distilleries in

The *Theologian* Slave Trader

Copenhagen. Thus, the indirect return journey from the Guinea Coast took several dangerous months.

Because of the conditions at the fort for the Europeans, coupled with the fact that there were very few Danish women transported, the Administration was given permission from Copenhagen to allow Danish men to marry village women living around the fort. Although, many European traders took this opportunity to marry local, African women and had children, such marriages were just marriages of convenience, often misusing and abusing these children, without much respect for them. The Dutch slave trader, William Bosmann, for example, described the Mulatto "race" in the late seventeenth century thus:

> The whole brood, when young, are far from handsome, and when old, are only fit to fright children to beds. If a Painter were obliged to paint Envy, I could wish him no better Original to draw after than an old Mulatto Woman ... But I shall here leave them for fear it may be thought that I am prejudiced by hatred against 'em', but so far from that, that there is not a single Person who hath anything to do with them, but he must own they are not worth speaking to. (Bosman, no date)

Despite all these difficulties on the coast, the Danes were not deterred. King Frederik IV issued a decree that those soldiers, who wanted to go to the Guinea Coast to protect Danish Forts and Danish trading activities, could be commissioned for ten years. Thus, a young eighteen year old farmhand, called Henrik Petersen, from Ballum, South Jutland, enrolled in the army. After serving, first at Ribe, Southwest Jutland, and also a few places on Zealand, Henrik was commissioned to go and serve on the Guinea Coast. Petersen arrived at Christiansborg Fort in 1708 at the age of about 21 years. He quickly found himself a young village girl, from one of the mud and stick farm houses at the village of Teshi, not far from the village of Osu. All the villagers were considered heathens, although they had their own belief system with their own priests and priestesses. They served God, the Creator, through their ancestral spirits as well as through lesser gods. Henrik had to convert his wife to Christianity, a religion that nobody in the village really understood. As a result, the teenage girl was very quickly baptised by the Fort's Lutheran pastor, Johannes Rask, and she was given the Danish name Margrethe.

The couple had four children, one of them a boy, born in 1710, was given the name Frederik Petersen. Henrik Petersen then built a hut in the village of Osu for his family, where he spent his free time when off duty from Christiansborg. Unfortunately, in 1717 after being on the coast for a remarkable eight and a half years, Henrik died suddenly from one of the climatic fevers. He was buried in the fort's cemetery. Margrethe, at the age of twenty-four, together with her extended heathen family members, had to take care of the baptised children.

From this period, conditions at Christiansborg went from bad to worse for the Danish Christian people. In 1720, the new Danish Governor at the fort was Peter Ostrup who had come to relieve Knud Rost. His task was to try and restructure the whole business. Even the fort's church, for example, was in ruins. This aspect of the general decline of the fort explained why the Pastor, Elias Svane, left Copenhagen on the Company's ship, *Haabets Galley*, on the 18th of August 1721. He had a very grand send off from the company officials and shareholders. They hoped that his prayers and diligence could give moral support to the establishment and thereby help the traders to work hard in order to increase the number of slaves for shipment. Together with the pastor on the ship were new traders, officers, soldiers and sailors. Before Svane's ship reached Christiansborg, he wrote a letter to be sent home to his sister, saying that, by the grace of God, their ship had picked up many slaves along the West African coast even before they got to Christiansborg Fort. Finally, on the 12th of January 1722, Svane and all the various officials and trading representatives, soldiers and the others coming to work at the fort, landed to a tumultuous welcome.

An important part of Svane's mission, besides church services at the fort, was to collect as many Mulatto boys as possible, teach them Christianity, the Danish language and Latin. He also was involved in training the boys to be soldiers and guards. Frederik Petersen, who was still living with his mother's family after his father's death, was then, at the age of ten, one of these boys, who had been enrolled as a child soldier and, later on, to study the bible at the church school.

Svane found the young Frederik to be tall and muscular, handsome and strong, as well as being very clever, hard working, loyal, full of a good sense of humour and highly intelligent. However, he also found that the boy had a fiery temperament. These characteristics were of significant importance during his life's journey. The impressed pastor then adopted Frederik as his son in order to take him back to Denmark. Therefore, by a twist of good fortune, in 1727 at the age of about 17, Frederik sailed with his new father, Svane, once Svane had finished his mission on the coast. They sailed on the ship, *Haabets Galley* with 248 African slaves chained and locked up in the small hull of the ship.

On the night before sailing, there was a send off party at the village of Osu, for Frederik, to wish him God's protection and blessings. There were great fires at Osu village, outside the fort, surrounded by drummers, dancers and singers, attended by Frederik, his African family and all the villagers. (See Sørensen, 1992.) Some of them wailed fearfully, as nobody knew the sort of destiny awaiting the young man in the land of the white-man.

Farewell dancing

The next day, the Danish captain, Lorentz Span, set sail. Frederik experienced a difficult journey. The conditions under which the slaves were being transported were awful. The young man could only look on. Every now and then, the doors of the hold were unlocked and opened for a little fresh air to come in. The stench from faeces, urine, vomit, blood and even dead bodies, which pervaded the entire ship, was unbearable. It was often so bad, that the sailors had to fetch buckets of sea water to pour over the slaves - men, women, young boys, young-girls - all naked, in order to minimise the filthy, sweating, stench.

There were no babies as they had been thrown on the beach as their mothers were being rowed to the ship. Whenever the hull doors were opened, the naked people could be seen, their shouting and screaming heard. Some of them, sad and confused, would still refuse to move around or hop or dance for exercise when the sailors played their fiddles. This, in turn, made the angry sailors flog the slaves with long whips, as they swore and called them "black satans" or "brown apes". The whipping would make all the slaves dance in the end. Svane often told his seventeen year old son, not to look at them while they were whipped. But Frederik, who was busy continuing his schooling, studying Latin, Greek, Hebrew, The New Testament and Danish on the ship, could not help but watch these tragic daily scenes and feel deeply depressed.

Sometimes, slaves were thrown into the ocean alive because a lack of winds which caused the ships to take longer to reach their destinations caused serious food and water shortages onboard. Fortunately, on Frederik's journey there were very good winds, therefore only the dead slaves were thrown into the shark infested waters. However, the bodies of sailors and other Danish officials who died onboard the ship were neatly prepared and Svane prayed to Jesus Christ to welcome their souls for judgement day. These Christian bodies were carefully, and respectfully, lowered into the sea. At the end of the crossing to Europe, on this particular journey, eight Danes and twenty-one slaves had died, leaving 227 slaves alive who were sold in the West Indies for profit.

CHAPTER 8
FREDERIK ON THE HAABETS GALLEY TO DENMARK VIA THE WEST INDIES

Pastor Elias Svane and his son, Frederik Petersen Svane, left the Guinea Coast on the 6th of March 1727 and luckily reached the island of St Thomas, Danish West Indies, after three months at sea. The *Haabets Galley* was the same ship on which the pastor arrived at Christiansborg fort, five years earlier. The slaves on board had to be sold to plantation owners on St Thomas, St Jan and the French island of St Croiz. Then molasses had to be bought and loaded onto the *Haabets Galley* before she could continue to Copenhagen. This meant that Frederik, his father and other Danish passengers, had to remain on St Thomas for some time and had to witness the bidding at the slave market.

Because of the coming sale, just before they were put on land at St Thomas, the slaves were well fed with large portions of maize or millet porridge, as well as vegetables and fruits, which were quickly brought on board the ship. Then they were well cleaned and smeared with palm oil in the traditional manner. On the beach where they landed was a magnificent fort. This fort was situated in the beautiful town of Charlotte Amalie. The resident Danish Lutheran Pastor, Ole Nicolaisen, whose mission there was to take care of the spiritual wellbeing of the plantation owners, came to greet Svane and his son. They were also warmly welcomed by his Danish wife and their three children. Nicolaisen lived in a beautiful mansion amongst other gorgeous villas in the town which were all serviced by household African slaves.

At last the slave cargo was unloaded, put into small rowing boats with the slaves' feet fastened with heavy iron chains and, with the Danish soldiers, rowed ashore and put into holding cells at the fort. On the day of the auction, customers who were mostly plantation owners, and slave merchants from the Danish islands, as well as from other neighbouring European islands, came to the fort. One of these traders told Elias and Frederik that some of the small islands around St Thomas were deserted, whereas some already had wild run-away slaves living on their own in freedom.

On the day of the auction, slaves with their heavy foot-chains were fenced in the market area of the fort. The first batch to be auctioned was a group of the best young men: good muscles, strong arms and buttocks, strong chests and good teeth. Their heavy metal foot-chains were attached to heavy tree trunks, lying beside them, as they lay on the ground. But soon, as part of the inspection, the male slaves had to get up and jump up and down in the burning sun. These men fetched very good prices between 180 and 270 Danish *Rigsdaler* (old Danish currency). The older men, women, children and teenagers also had to go through similar inspection after the main sale.

When the auction was over, the owners of the bought slaves tied their new property behind their wagons pulled by horses or donkeys. The slaves walked behind the wagons as they were led to their owners' homes. The slaves lived in mud houses behind their masters' impressive mansions. Frederik was told by their hosts that every day the male slaves worked on the plantations, while the women and the child slaves worked in the houses. Some of the women and girls also became mistresses of their male owners behind the backs of their European wives.

During the time they stayed at the Vicarage in the town of Charlotte Amalie, Frederik used to go for walks on the main street and along the beach called Dronningens Gade - Queen's Street. On many of these walks, he witnessed scenes of cruelty to the Africans such as: chained slaves fastened to wagons being whipped by their masters; the Danish owners calling out as they flogged the poor men, "you Black devils" or "you Black monkeys". (Sørensen, 1992)

After three weeks, the *Haabets Galley*, cleaned and loaded with molasses, tobacco, cotton, rum, and lignum vitae, and with all her Danish passengers on board, set sail again and left St Thomas, heading towards Copenhagen. Judging from how quiet the young Frederik had become, the five month travelling experience before reaching Denmark had already made a deeply negative, psychological mark on him.

CHAPTER 9
GODSON OF HIS MAJESTY, KING FREDERIK IV

At last, Pastor Elias Svane and his half African son arrived in Copenhagen, where they presented themselves to His Excellency, Duke Carl Adolph von Plessen, the director of the West Indian-Guinean Company. Von Plessen immediately sent a message to King Frederik IV about the sensation of the heathen, half African boy, who had just arrived in Copenhagen. His Majesty invited them for an audience without delay. Svane then presented his adopted son to the King. His Majesty was very impressed. He ordered the boy to be baptised without delay and he announced that he would be Frederik's Godfather. The baptism took place with pomp and ceremony in Copenhagen's grand and sumptuous *Garnisonnskirken* at Sankt Anne Plads and was attended by royalty, aristocrats and important citizens. One of the significant baptismal gifts from the guests was a promise by Von Plessen, who later became Prime Minister for the Danish-Norwegian Kingdom, that the West Indian-Guinean Company was prepared to pay for Frederik's education, including his university education.

Ironically, at this time, arguments and discussions were taking place in Copenhagen amongst anxious shareholders concerned with their trade on the Guinea Coast. This anxiety was in connection with news which had just arrived with the ship *Haabets Galley*. The key concern was how to find ways to increase the total number of the slaves being shipped each year. This in effect meant, firstly, how to find ways and means to stimulate fighting amongst the African tribes in order to generate more black prisoners of war. Secondly, how to encourage clans to increase their reproduction to ensure that there would never be a shortage of new child slaves. Finally, they were thinking about how their company's shares could increase in value. One of the problems facing the company was that, even though the slaves were acquired very cheaply from the Guinea Coast, and then sold at much higher prices in the West Indies, the cost of the shipment, and also considering the fact that many slaves died during the transportation, made actual profit margins very thin. Many shareholders became dissatisfied over time. So notable figures such as the Baron, Professor Ludvig Holberg, sold their stock in the company.

While these arguments and discussions were going on in Copenhagen, Svane was offered a job as a pastor at a parish with two little churches: Sorterup and Ottestrup on Zealand island, south west of Copenhagen. The young pastor formerly in charge had died suddenly. So Svane and Frederik, moved to the little Sorterup vicarage, with its beautiful whitewashed church. Svane employed a young housekeeper, a pastor's daughter, whom he later married.

While Frederik wandered about the village that first winter, he saw more white-skinned children as well as heavy snow. He had to put on heavy clothing and heavy wooden shoes. Frederik's presence in the village caused a sensation and a lot of gossiping in all the surrounding villages too. Sørensen (1992) describes how people stared at him wherever he went - at his curly hair, brown skin, brown eyes, his thick lips and his not so sharp nose. He spoke Danish with a strange accent, and claimed that he was the son of the white pastor, and that His Majesty, King Frederik IV was his Godfather! Sometimes, Frederik had the opportunity to accompany his father to some of the important meetings that were being held at the Manor House, Odemark, where the two churches lay. During the grand dinners, Sørensen (ibid) describes how Frederik could not understand the important people and their discussions about falling or rising profits in the black commodity, while they looked over and smiled at him.

CHAPTER 10
FREDERIK'S EDUCATION

At the age of 17, Frederik and a handful of local boys started their formal education at the vicarage. Unsurprisingly, his father being the teacher, Frederick was far ahead in his education in most of the subjects. The main disciplines at the time were: Latin, Hebrew, geography, history, Greek and Danish. Later on, Frederik continued his schooling by going to a larger school at Slagelse, the biggest town in the area, south west of Copenhagen. Frederik used to walk many kilometres daily from Sorterup to this school and back home again.

From his first day, Frederik started to have problems with his classmates, especially some of the local boys from Sorterup. He was extremely clever, tall, handsome and very strong but he did not like fighting. Frederik was often attacked physically by a large gang of boys who teased, mobbed and then gave him very nasty nicknames like: "son of a bitch", "you arrogant nigger" or "you brown monkey" (Søresnen, 1992). This verbal abuse and teasing, as well as the serious physical attacks, was carried out by his new classmates and the older boys at the Slagelse school. Despite the constant abuse, Frederik persevered and passed all his exams. He was then admitted to Copenhagen University as a theology student in 1732. He was quiet and lonely and was not really accepted socially by his fellow Danish students. His Professor was the well-known writer, poet and Baron, Ludvig Holberg. The Rector-Magnificus, was a well-known author of books on Latin, metaphysics, philosophy, theology and history. All university lectures at the time were given in Latin.

Frederik lived in one of the rooms in the students' residence near the university called the *Regensen*, which was in central Copenhagen. He worked hard but did not socialise much with the other students, although he was felt to be a decent enough person. At this period of time, many Danes had not seen an African or a Mulatto before, so his room mate, a theology student called Christian Albertsen Bogvad, also a son of a pastor, wrote to his parents about his strange looking and lonely room mate who was now calling himself *Fredericus Petri Svane Africanus*:

'The strangest thing about this student is that, he just has brown complexion and strange dark wool on his head just like you see on our spring-lambs in the fields at home. He has told me that, the reason is that he was born in the hot sun in Africa and that his father has been a pastor for the Danish people at a fort called Christiansborg.' (Sørensen, 1992)

CHAPTER 11
FREDERICUS THE PIETIST

Gradually, Fredericus was being affected by his loneliness; he was the only mixed race person at the University, perhaps also in the whole of Copenhagen, with its 70,000 strong population. He could not fit into the Danish way of life. Consequently, in 1734, he joined the Pietists, a Christian evangelical movement in Copenhagen. He did this partly to get closer to Danes from all walks of life and partly to strengthen his faith in God. The major principle of this sect was to question the established Lutheran church's explanation of the so-called 'Will of God' which was taken for granted in Denmark. Thus the sect's aim in Christianity was described as 'experience and practices'.

There were quite a number of aristocratic dignitaries in Copenhagen who became members of the Pietist sect. Examples included: Ole Hersleb, brother of the Royal Pastor Peder Hersleb; the radical pastor, Enevold Ewald; and a well-known widow called Madam Maria Wulf. Thus, Fredericus and two other theology students, as well as a few other students from the university, became members.

Eventually, the movement started to grow. Many pastors from all over Denmark became converts, also churchmen from Sweden, notably Pastor Jacob Emesson. Many intellectuals in Copenhagen, as well as many people from the poorer sections of Danish society, became members. Meetings were held at Madam Wulf's apartment, which was in the centre of Copenhagen and not far from the students' residence. The King himself was sympathetic but was careful not to take sides because the Pietist sermons were very critical of the Bishop of Zealand and the established Danish Lutheran Church, whose head was the King.

As these activities in which Fredericus became deeply committed gathered momentum, it was revealed that Fredericus had become involved with a girl, who was once a member, but had left the movement to work as a prostitute. Fredericus had to live with the consequences of this shocking revelation. Unfortunately, he made things worse for himself. He started another relationship with another young woman from the Pietist congregation. After they had been together for a short time, it turned out that she was an aristocrat's daughter. This woman therefore was quickly married to a suitor from another aristocratic family, arranged by her mother and father. Fredericus could do nothing about this intervention.

In order to fulfil his ambition of becoming a cleric in the Lutheran Church, Fredericus had to pass his final university examination. As the Bishop in Copenhagen and many of his conservative bishops were against this new Pietist movement, towards the end of 1734 the Bishop was given a number of names of theology students who were known Pietists who were due to take their final oral examination. These students, including Fredericus, were summoned to a special hearing and, at their final examination, they were asked to denounce the sect in order to become members of the established church. When it came to his turn, and to the surprise and annoyance of the examining professors and clerics, Fredericus gave a spirited lecture condemning the conservatism of the Danish bishops. He condemned their interpretation of the 'Will of God' thesis and their understanding of the New Testament as a whole. He then outlined his criticism of the Bishops' way of life, their clothes, their accommodation, and their social conduct in general!

Naturally Fredericus, despite being an outstanding student, was asked to apologise for his criticisms in order to get his final university degree. Again, he made his situation more difficult by refusing to apologise. He received support from the dignitaries and the radical pastors of his congregation. Some of his fellow theology students also wrote to their families about what was happening to Fredericus. Despite this support, Fredericus was expelled from Copenhagen University. He was also removed from the university residence at the *Regensen*. Worse still, all his financial support from the West Indian-

Guinea Company ceased. In the end, all the pastors and students who refused to leave the Pietist movement were either suspended or sacked from their positions.

In December 1734, he went home to his father for Christmas. He explained to Svane what had been happening to him in Copenhagen and the consequences. His father was very upset and furious with the young man, and instructed his son to go back to apologise to the examination board. Fredericus refused his father's request and said that he would not. Consequently, Svane cut all ties with his adopted son and announced he did not want to see Fredericus ever again.

After the terrible breakdown of his family at Christmas, Fredericus returned to Copenhagen, poor and homeless. He contacted his congregation for help. Two of the members offered support. The first was a Mr Piper who was in charge of the King's Orphanage in Copenhagen. He offered Fredericus meals twice a day at the orphanage. The second person was a very poor carpenter, who offered him a room in Fiolstraede, in the middle of Copenhagen. Eventually, Piper was sacked from his work for refusing to attend Holy Communion services.

Seven years after his arrival in Denmark, Fredericus at his lowest point, was forced to beg for help. In the year 1734 he wrote:

> 'Now I have been excluded from human help; motherless and fatherless in this country, but God is my helper. I will go back as a second Apostle Paul, to help my "heathen and blind" people to see God's Light ....' (Sørensen, 1992)

CHAPTER 12
FREDERICUS THE MISSIONARY

Fredericus realised that he had no future in Denmark. He decided to go back to the Guinea Coast as 'a second Paul', to convert his people from Heathenism to Christianity and to help redeem their souls. Before he embarked on his new mission, Fredericus decided to rush to his father, at Sorterup Vicarage, to explain to him his latest plans. On his way there, as he arrived at Slagelse, he went to the house of Catharina Maria Badsch and her parents to greet them. Catharina was a young teenage girl he used to know during his school days in Slagelse. One time, when Fredericus was attacked by a group of some of his classmates and was badly beaten and wounded, he had taken refuge in her parents' house. As soon as Fredericus entered their house, he told Catharina that he was going to go to Africa as a missionary and asked her whether she would marry him. Catharina said "yes" and that she wanted to go with him to Africa. Fredericus then announced his engagement to the girl's parents who, naturally, were a little confused. He then continued his walk home to Sorterup and immediately informed his father about the engagement and that he would be leaving Denmark for the Guinea Coast.

Pastor Svane and his wife, Sara, did not receive Fredericus cordially at all. Svane, who had already broken off the relationship with his son over events at the university, was furious. His opinion was that, Catharina Maria, being uneducated as well as the daughter of a German artisan immigrant, was below his dignity. Fredericus again ignored his father. He went back to Slagelse and married Catharina in a rushed ceremony. After the wedding he called his new wife by the name Trina. Both then hurried to Copenhagen in April 1735 where some friends from the Pietists found them temporary accommodation, while Fredericus tried to borrow some money for food, clothing and travel expenses for the journey to Africa.

The *Theologian* Slave Trader

As none of Fredericus's Pietist sect members would give him a loan for such a large amount, he contacted Adolph von Plessen, director of the West Indian-Guinean Company, for a loan. In the first instance, von Plessen offered Fredericus a job at Christiansborg Fort rather than an unconditional loan. Fredericus refused the offer, explaining that he had made up his mind to go to the coast as a missionary, to convert his poor people so that they would go to the Kingdom of God when they died. This zeal seemed to do the trick and Fredericus was not forced to take the proposed company job. He was given a loan to buy clothes for himself and his wife. They were also offered the passage and the food on ship, on the company's credit.

The ship left Copenhagen in May 1735 and reached Christiansborg Fort after twelve weeks sailing. Her cargo was the normal load of weapons, passengers and Danish schnapps. The fort's new officials, soldiers and sailors disembarked and were rowed in little local fishing boats to land. Fredericus and Trina set foot on the beach without money, without food and without even basic accommodation for that night.

Fortunately for Fredericus, he met on the ship an old school friend, a Mulatto soldier called Servin, who had been visiting Copenhagen on business. Fredericus told his friend about his mission, and that he and his wife had no food to eat that day and nowhere to sleep. Servin immediately offered to give Fredericus and his wife a room, upstairs in his house, just outside the fort. The house was near where the fort's servants' quarters were and Servin's wife, a young Mulatto woman, would serve them food once a day. They agreed that the board and lodging would all be on Servin's credit until Fredericus found work to pay his debts. Servin could offer this as he worked at the fort, sometimes as a policeman, an interpreter, a clerk or as a slave trader.

That first evening, Christiansborg Fort was teaming with life: drinking, eating, music and a wild party welcomed the newly arrived from Denmark. But Fredericus and his wife also had a warm welcome from the villagers at Osu. Many of them recognised Fredericus and welcomed him back and they drank, not schnapps, but lots of palm wine served in calabashes to celebrate his return. His old mother, Margrethe, his two sisters and a younger brother, Constable Johan Ditlev, were also on hand to enjoy the celebration and meet his new wife.

The next day, Søren Schielderup, a Norwegian, who also travelled with the ship, was sworn in as the new Counsellor Governor by the Pastor Eric Trane in a church service at the fort's chapel. Immediately after this ceremony, a soldier was sent to Servin's house to fetch Fredericus to the fort. There he was told the amount of money he owed the company for their clothes, the journey and the food he and his wife ate during the twelve weeks' sailing. His debt was calculated at 20 *Rigsdaler* for clothes and journey and 12 *Rigsdaler* for food on the ship. He was asked to pay the 32 *Rigsdaler* he owed that very moment. The shocked Fredericus tried to explain about the agreement reached with the director in Copenhagen but he was not given chance to explain. Fredericus's new set of clothes, were seized in place of 20 *Rigsdaler*, and Trina's two dresses and a handful of their things for 12 *Rigsdaler*, totalling 32 *Rigsdaler*, exactly the amount of money he owed the company.

After this episode, Fredericus and his wife, Trina, had to take refuge in his mother's and other family members' houses to eat some of their meals there. Trina learned very quickly how to make some of the local dishes like *kenkey* which was fermented maize dough formed into round balls and steamed, then served with very strong fish soup or stew. However, they had no money to buy the ingredients so that they had to rely on the family's generosity, while they continued to eat once a day the food given them by Servin's wife.

However, the problems of Fredericus and his wife were becoming more complicated every day. Servin was becoming worried that Fredericus and his wife would never be able to pay what they owed him. Therefore, one day he had a long discussion with Fredericus in which Servin pointed out to him that first, as a highly educated intelligent person who had been to university, he should realise that his heathen people would never give up their religion to follow Christianity. Servin argued that the so called, 'good' Christians at the fort were daily engaged in prostitution, drunkenness, theft, rape and endless quarrelling. Given their maltreatment of the house slaves as well, how could this possibly be a good example of Christianity for the villagers to follow?

Secondly, Servin asked Fredericus whether he thought these villagers could afford to pay him enough money to buy food and also pay for

The *Theologian* Slave Trader

his accommodation. Servin wondered why Fredericus turned down the offer for a job with the company just before he started his journey from Copenhagen. Why had he not been clever enough to just accept the offer for the time being? In the end, Servin offered to buy Trina from him for 80 *Rigsdaler*, plus an extra 50 *Rigsdaler* to clear his debts. Completely shaken, Fredericus said nothing but rushed to their room, fetched his wife and fled from Servin's house. Constable Johan Ditlev, Fredericus's younger brother took them into his modest hut, where his wife, Elizabeth, prepared a mat for her brother-in-law and sister-in law to sleep on.

After a long discussion with Johan Ditlev, exploring all the possibilities of finding employment for Trina, Trina herself offered to take any odd jobs such as doing laundry work at the fort, or mending clothes and socks, patching, ironing clothes or cooking, as she was used to such work back home in Denmark. Fredericus, however, disagreed for two reasons: first, he thought that such a housemaid's job for his wife was below his dignity; second, he felt it was the husband who should earn a living for his family.

Eventually, Trina contacted Madam Helena Trane, the Pastor's wife at the fort, who welcomed Trina with great joy after Counsellor Governor Søren Schielderup had approved of such work at the fort. Fredericus, on the other hand, obstinately insisted that he had come as a missionary to redeem the souls of his people. So he started to translate the New Testament from Greek to Ga, the local language. However, his attempt was considered ridiculous as Trina's wages were not enough to buy their food. Moreover, the villagers did not understand his intentions. His biblical translation was so poor and he could not find correct Ga words for the Greek version of the Holy Bible.

Finally, Fredericus overcame his own obstinacy and gave up his mission. He went to Christiansborg Fort to ask the governor for employment. This was further forced on him as Trina became pregnant and could not do the heavy work, such as the laundry work. She would have to stop work altogether at some point. However, right until the end of her pregnancy, she continued to work, taking on light duties like mending and patching rather than the washing of clothes.

Although Counsellor Governor Søren Schielderup had seized all his belongings, Fredericus thought that Schielderup had high morals and conducted himself ethically. This showed in the way he was organising the everyday activities at the fort, the church's role, as well as the careful monitoring and controlling of fair trading practices and the behaviour of both the Danes and the African slave suppliers.

Eventually this Governor became very popular amongst both the Europeans and the Africans who had business contacts with the Fort. Sometimes some Africans, not necessarily traders, came from inland just to look at him. One of the powerful kings far away in the interior of the land sent a delegation with his beautiful young daughter to be presented to the governor just to make her pregnant and then send her back. Schielderup, however, stood by his Christian moral code and sent her back without sleeping with her. Whilst he showed great respect for humanity, paradoxically, Schielderup personally exchanged Danish and Norwegian weapons, axes, knives and colourful clothing for slaves and, with heavy iron chains, sent them to the fort's inhuman dungeons before shipment. Another paradox was that he hated African women. On his orders, all the African and Mulatto women and girls, whether they were wives, mistresses or prostitutes, were removed from the fort into the village.

Fredericus had no choice but to seek urgent help from Schielderup. Before their meeting, Fredericus had acquired another loan to be able to pay his debt at the fort. Before opening his mouth to speak, the governor reached into a drawer and brought out some documents outlining Fredericus's behaviour during interviews at the university, his condemnation of the official Christian Lutheran Church of the Kingdom of Denmark-Norway, and the amount of money he owed. The Governor was very sarcastic throughout the whole meeting but told Fredericus that there was a ship with the influential Captain Grøn, coming to land very soon. He would discuss the matter with him. Fredericus left very disappointed.

Fredericus, however, had a second plan. He headed straight to see Pastor Trane and pleaded with him to help him find some work. The pastor advised him to write an application for employment rather

The *Theologian* Slave Trader

than just ask. Trane also wrote a kind letter of recommendation, saying how clever Fredericus was at the university, and attached this reference to the application letter, which was delivered the same day to the governor's office.

In the early spring of 1736, Trina delivered a baby boy, who was christened Elias Frederiksen Svane by Pastor Trane within a few days. Both the pastor and the governor came with gifts to congratulate Fredericus and Trina. Finally, on April 2nd 1736, Captain Grøn and the ship *Jomfruen* arrived on the Guinea coast outside Christiansborg Fort. After all the formalities and the festivities, both the captain and the governor studied Fredericus's application. Both of them were highly impressed. They now realised that Fredericus was an excellent writer, as well as appearing to be a true scholar. He was offered employment immediately as parish clerk and a teacher at the fort. Fredericus, Trina and baby Elias, moved on the same day from the hut where they had been lodging to an empty room in the 'rank and file' quarters of the fort.

Fredericus and his wife had another twist of good fortune. All the clothes and the few belongings that had been seized by order of the governor, were given back to them. With regard to the 32 *Rigsdaler* that they owed, Fredericus was told that a small amount of money would be deducted from his salary every month towards the payment of this debt. So Fredericus started work the following day, helping the pastor and also trying to persuade some Mulatto children from Osu village to come to the school. While only a handful turned up, he started to teach them Christianity and Danish.

Fredericus also worked as a writer and a translator for the buyers and sellers of slaves, alcoholic drinks and weapons. He gradually became more and more deeply involved in the slave trading activities at the fort. Paradoxically, because of this new role, Fredericus became good friends with Governor Schielderup. Trina was also trying hard to cope, taking care of little Elias as well as being a housewife; at the same time she continued to do light work, like mending clothes for the people at the fort. So, while life was a little better after 1736, they were both still very poor.

CHAPTER 13
TRINA IS SEDUCED

On the 14th of June 1736, Governor Schielderup died suddenly of the 'climatic fever' that was killing many Danes at the fort that summer. Immediately, a senior Norwegian bookkeeper named Enevold Nielsen Boris was appointed the next governor. Boris had been at the fort for over five years so he had some experience and was also known to be highly efficient at his job. As soon as he became governor, Boris cancelled all Fredericus and Trina's debts. This was very welcome at first. Unfortunately, Boris had a strong personal reason for helping the couple with their debt problem. The governor started to take an interest in Trina and began to deliver gifts, including nice ladies' clothes, to her when Fredericus was out working.

Boris had once had a local girlfriend but the late governor, Schielderup, had forced all the local girls and young women to leave the fort. Thus, Boris' girlfriend had left him to go and live with her family in the village. Trina though was extremely happy with the lovely Danish women's clothes she was receiving. The gifts continued to arrive at her door. In the end, Fredericus found out and confronted his wife. He warned her not to entertain Boris nor accept any gifts when he was not at home.

Finally though, Trina who had had enough of her poor husband went berserk with anger, shouting and screaming and smashing objects in their room. (See Søresnen, 1992) She accused Fredericus of being, 'narrow minded' and putting them in such a difficult situation. She blamed him for refusing to finish his final examination in order to qualify as a pastor; joining a crazy, Christian sect; refusing to accept the job at the fort which was offered to him before leaving

The *Theologian* Slave Trader

Copenhagen and borrowing money that he could not repay. Trina left their room in anger, leaving the baby behind and went to the balcony near the governor's residence. While she was standing under the balcony crying, Boris saw her, brought her in his residence and they spent the night together.

The next day when Fredericus was at work, Boris instructed his household slaves to go and fetch Trina's belongings and the child. Trina lived with the governor from that day on. Unfortunately, during the evening of the day that Trina left, events went from bad to worse. Pastor Trane rushed to knock at Fredericus's door crying and saying that his beloved wife, Helena, had just died. He explained that he needed help to find somebody in the village with a ready made coffin. Both men were in great shock but managed to make some plans for the funeral, which took place the next day. At the funeral, which was conducted partly by the confused pastor and partly by a very unhappy Fredericus, Boris and Trina arrived hand in hand. Trina, with her new clothes and lovely hairdo looked beautiful and happy. The next day, the sad and still confused Trane asked the company establishment to release him from his job. He started to pack his belongings ready to leave the coast with the next ship bound for Copenhagen via the West Indies.

Almost everyday, Fredericus saw Trina walking around the fort but they never talked to each other. As more and more weeks went by, Trina started to look miserable when Fredericus saw her. Eventually, when the governor was not at the fort, Fredericus met Trina on one of the fort's battlements. Trina started to cry and held her husband's hand complaining that she could not live with the governor any longer for he was a wicked man. She told Fredericus that, every night, Boris brought prostitutes to his residence. She explained that she wanted to come back to him. But Fredericus could not bring himself to say anything, instead he went to consult Trane and ask him what to do. His main concern was that he did not want to bring yet more disgrace upon himself by accepting Trina back. But Trane was too depressed over the death of his wife to give him any sensible advice. Fredericus then took a firm decision himself. He would send Trina and their child back to Denmark, on board the next available ship.

Trina agreed that it was for the best and went to tell the governor, when he came back from his visit outside the fort, that she wanted to leave for Denmark. Surprisingly, Boris was so happy to get rid of her and her baby, that he ordered free passage for them at once on the next available ship. When she got her travel papers, Pastor Trane promised Fredericus that he would take care of the two of them as he was going on the same ship. Kindly, Trane also promised to hand them over to Pastor Svane, technically Trina's father-in-law, at Sorterup as soon as they got back to Denmark.

One fine day, in the spring of 1738, Fredericus stood on one of the fort's battlements, overlooking the ocean, to watch his estranged wife and his son waiting on the beach ready to be rowed to the ship *Laarburg Galley*. After hundreds of heavily chained slaves: men, women, young boys, young girls, had been brought out of their dungeons underneath the fort and rowed to the ship, the Danish and Norwegian passengers from the fort, were rowed gently to the ship, anchored about two hundred metres away. Fredericus stood quietly to watch this personal tragedy. After three years of his missionary nightmare, he watched the *Laarburg Galley* moving away slowly with his broken family and his oldest friend.

After six months, the ship reached Copenhagen. Unfortunately, Pastor Trane, along with some of the slaves and Danes and Norwegians on board the ship, had died onboard long before they had even reached the West Indies. In Copenhagen that day, some of the Danes Trina had met on board the ship helped her to find a job as a housemaid in Copenhagen, as she again had no money. After some months as a housemaid, and when she could afford to pay for the journey, Trina continued to her father-in-law's at the Sorterup vicarage. Elias Svane, now a widower, received her with mixed feelings but he was very happy to receive his grandson, Elias. At the vicarage Trina spent her time working as a housemaid for the old man.

CHAPTER 14
FREDERICUS THE SLAVE TRADER

Fredericus was gradually coming to terms with his destiny. He tried to avoid confrontation with Governor Boris. This was vital as Boris was his employer and had the power to throw him out of the fort if he wished. The first thing he did after Trina and Elias had left was to find new friends and allies. One such friend was Ludvig Ferdinand Romer, a twenty-five-year old soldier, who kept order for the slave merchants. As well as his guard duties, Romer was a slave trader himself. He was fairly new at the fort and had a beautiful young African wife from the interior.

The next person Fredericus moved closer to was the fort's sergeant and translator called Cornelius Petersen. He had arrived at Christiansborg eighteen years earlier when he was only seventeen years old. He was therefore regarded as the man who had served at the fort for the longest time. Petersen had learned the local Ga language and had also lived with many local girls. At the age of 35, he looked like a 50 year-old man. He called his most recent wife Anna Sophie after the old Danish Queen. Fredericus had got to know Petersen as he had been promoted to a sergeant in charge of the training of the Mulatto child soldiers.

Fredericus started to enjoy a new life with his friends now that Trina and Elias were gone. With some peace of mind, most evenings, Fredericus and Romer would go to the local villages of Osu, Labadi and Teshi, not far from the fort, to visit friends and family. Usually they would dress up in their elegant European clothes and would bring a few gifts with them to enjoy themselves with local girls and drink alcohol. Romer, although married, kept a local girl called Ingeborg who gave birth to a baby girl. Fredericus also bought himself a slave girl he called Mette.

Romer only bought particular types of slaves; usually young women with children, very young boys and young girls from approximately eleven or twelve years old. These ages fetched very good prices at the market. In regard to his purchases, there was one particular incident that Fredericus watched with great interest at the fort. One day a young man and his equally young wife from the interior Akwamu district, which was far away from the coast, came to see the various Danish goods for sale, out of curiosity. He was introduced by mistake to Romer as a trader. But Romer became irritated when he found out that these two people had not come to buy or sell anything. The next thing that happened was that Romer asked some of his soldiers to invite the 'monkey' out for a drink. The man's wife was left behind on her own.

After some time, the young man returned, completely drunk and unable to balance or walk properly. He asked for his wife who, unfortunately, had ended up in the slave-dungeon. The distraught young man could not find her anywhere. He went amok, screaming, while he looked for his wife, so Romer's security guards bound him up and threw him out of the fort, slamming the gates behind him. Romer then offered this young woman to Fredericus, to use her as a sex slave, until the next ship arrived for loading cargo.

Fredericus's other friend and ally, Cornelius Petersen, decided to make a nice vegetable and fruit garden at the fort. It was an idea that he and Boris had once had when they had visited the main English slave fort at Cape Coast west of Christiansborg. This peaceful time even saw Fredericus come to like the governor. Unfortunately for everyone at the fort, Boris died suddenly on the 6th of June 1740, after just four years as governor and after nine years trading on the coast. As usual, another governor was sworn in immediately. This person was the company's chief trader, Peter Nikolaj Jurgensen, who came to the coast in 1733. He had been in charge of the trading activities at Fredensborg Fort near the village of Store Ningo, about 75 km east of Christiansborg.

This appointment did not please Fredericus for he did not consider Jurgensen to be a satisfactory person to work for. Fredericus had this

The *Theologian* Slave Trader

attitude towards him because, as an administrator besides being the parish clerk and also a teacher, Fredericus was deeply involved in the business of buying and selling slaves and weapons, not only on behalf of the company, but also for himself. Therefore his official duties and his need to work closely with this new governor were getting in the way of his profitable slave trading. Fredericus was in charge of the church services, reading prayers and organising burials until a new pastor, Oluf Dorph, arrived. Unfortunately this pastor did not stay long. Dorph did not like his work and he left the fort to go back to Denmark in 1742; he was replaced by Pastor Peter Meyer.

Perhaps due to the lack of real Christian guidance from the centre, and the weakness of Jurgensen, morals amongst the entire Danish community gradually deteriorated. Nobody trusted anybody. There was disillusionment, drunkenness, gluttony, embezzlement, nervous break downs, fist fighting, prostitution, diseases, theft, rape and, of course, many deaths. Eventually the community at the fort divided into gangs; people had to blockade themselves in their rooms at night for their own safety.

The result was that, for example, the company's book-keepers, Hans Hansen Blass and Simon Henriksen Klein, drank so much that they completely neglected their duties. Trader Romer and his deputy, August Frederik Hackenberg, cheated so much that they accumulated great fortunes for themselves. The new Pastor, Peter Meyer, who drank so much that on occasion he could not even remember his own name, joined the gang of Sergeant Petersen, who was well placed to fight as he was in charge of training the Mulatto child soldiers. These gangs had no respect whatsoever for Governor Jurgensen. In the end Jurgensen became so frightened that he drank vast amounts of cognac everyday. Isolated and helpless, he hated all the Danes at the fort except Fredericus.

CHAPTER 15
THE ASANTE KING, NANA OPOKU WARE INVADES THE COAST

Besides the internal instability of Christiansborg Fort, the administration was never strong enough to defend itself from the inland warlord invaders. One such invader, nearly fifty years earlier, was called Asameni, from the Kingdom of Akwamu. Asameni was once an important private trader and a good friend of the administration at Christiansborg. However, in 1693, he was able to trick the Danes at the fort; he brought about eighty men from Akwamu with him on the pretence that they were all buying weapons but, in the end, Asameni and his men turned the loaded guns they had been inspecting onto the surprised Danish salesmen. Asameni was then able to occupy the fort as the new governor for several months. Finally, administrators from other European forts had to come to Christiansborg and mediate. The humiliated Danes had to pay him a large sum of money to leave the fort and spare his captives.

When there was anarchy inside the fort later on, the events of 1693 were remembered. In the spring of 1742, the King of the Asante Kingdom, Nana Opoku Ware (Oware), with hundreds of his fierce warriors, came from far inland to invade all the villages and the European trading forts along the coast. These included the Dutch Fort Creveceur, the English St James Fort and the Danish Christiansborg Fort as well as all the smaller trading posts. The invaders looted and stole money, weapons, gold, and barrels of alcohol from the whole area. In addition to the looting, King Opoku Ware, demanded that the Danes send one important white man to come to their war camp on the Legon hills, situated north of Christiansborg Fort, to negotiate. Also, Nana Opoku Ware demanded that Fredericus had to come as an interpreter.

The *Theologian* Slave Trader

The fort's unlucky book-keeper, Blass, was sent to negotiate with Fredericus as his interpreter. The two men duly arrived at the King's encampment in the Legon hills. They were both dressed in their formal official Danish administrators' ceremonial attire. After the opening discussions, the King demanded to know whether a white man and a black man had similar physical bodies. Therefore, the shocked Blass was led to the King's private hut and was ordered to strip naked. Blass obeyed and some of the warriors, in the presence of the King, examined him from head to toe. They also examined his sexual organs, his anus, his armpits, his mouth, his ears, and counted the number of teeth he had. In the end Nana Opoku Ware was satisfied that Europeans and Africans have the same physical features. As was the tradition, he then gave Blass and Fredericus small gifts of some of the gold that had just been looted. Fredericus also received extra gifts of two very young boy and girl slaves. Then they were ordered to leave the camp that night. Unsurprisingly, Blass never forgot this episode and wanted to keep his humiliation secret from the people at the fort.

Before this episode, Fredericus had made little profit from his slave trading. Indeed he had again borrowed money, this time to buy some building materials, as he had decided to build himself a home at Osu village, just outside the fort. Fredericus had got it into his head that he was building the house for his wife Trina and son Elias who, for the time being, were far away. He hoped to be able to send for them one day and that they would return to the coast. In reality he did not even know what had happened to them.

More anarchy followed at the fort. During the height of this anarchy, Fredericus had tried to make peace among the various antagonistic gangs. But his move seriously backfired on him, mainly because of his ambitious house-building project. Many people at the fort became jealous of him and started to tell wild stories about his conspiracy with some of the interior Kings. The Danes claimed that Fredericus had conspired to overthrow the governor so that Christiansborg Fort would be closed down and all the slave trading transactions would be conducted at his new mansion, with him as the governor. The gift of the two slave children from the King only seemed to enhance these rumours. Eventually, almost everybody at the fort believed the story. Indeed, to make matters worse, Fredericus borrowed slaves from the fort, besides his own slaves, to work on his project so that the mansion would be finished as quickly as possible. In the end, he spent more time at his building site than at his administrative work.

One fine day, Fredericus heard that a French ship had arrived to buy slaves from Christiansborg. He hurried to make arrangements to sell his housemaid slave and sex partner Mette, the two young slave children and a few others. That day, high waves on the coast prevented the delivery of the slaves until later in the evening. By early evening Fredericus was on board the ship, had sold his slaves and entered into conversation with the French pastor on board. They spoke Latin together followed by many glasses of French Cognac. The next day, somewhat hung-over, Fredericus was arrested at his building site and sent to prison. He was then sent to the court house at Christiansborg where he was detained, charged two months' pay and even had his unfinished house confiscated.

CHAPTER 16
THE IMPRISONMENT OF FREDERICUS

Fredericus became so wild and angry at hearing this sentence which cost him his two months pay and the confiscation of his unfinished mansion building, that Governor Jurgensen became frightened and set him free. Despite this, his unfinished mansion remained confiscated, as did all his clothes, except those he was wearing. The court decided that he did indeed owe the money that he had borrowed from the company to buy the building materials from the fort's warehouse, and that he had also used some of it illegally to pay some local workers.

One evening after the hearing, Fredericus decided that he wanted to kill himself. But after meeting a depressed soldier, who was drinking heavily inside the fort, he joined the young man to drink away their sorrows. Fredericus got so drunk that he eventually staggered to Jurgensen's apartment and shouted that he was going to kill him. He was arrested and sent to the most secure dungeon the fort had to offer: the so called, 'Black Hole'. On occasions in the past when Fredericus had been arrested, being such a strong man, he had managed to break out of his chains in prison. During these incidents he had also threatened to kill not only Governor Jurgensen but the company's other leading officials as well: Hackenberg, Blass, Cornelius Petersen and even Pastor Meyer. However in this latest incident, Fredericus was thrown into prison, fastened with much heavier metal chains with spikes on; he was put on the bare floor with rats and mice running around, while stinking stagnated water dripped down from the ceiling.

There in the 'Black Hole' Fredericus lived for the next six months and was fed once a day on bread and water. Sores appeared all over his body, caused by the sharp teeth of the heavy metal chain spikes which tore at his clothes and into his flesh. While Fredericus was struggling in his dark cell, the book-keeper, Blass, was still very bitter about how the Asante King, Nana Opoku Ware, had humiliated him. He too was drinking very heavily and he also insulted Governor Jurgensen and threatened to kill him. Blass got so annoyed one day that he went to cut down all the fruit trees, flowers and other plants in the garden that he and Governor Boris had once planted. Becoming afraid of all these death threats, Jurgensen resigned and arranged to go back to Denmark. He asked Dorph, a trade representative at the Fredensborg Fort, to be governor at Christiansborg Fort. As soon as Dorph became the new governor, Fredericus was pardoned. Immediately, a blacksmith was brought from the village to saw the heavy metal chains off his body.

Governor Dorph made Fredericus promise not to seek revenge but to forgive everyone at the fort for all the wild rumours and the maltreatment he had endured through the previous six months. In return, Fredericus was given his post back as parish clerk and secretary to the administration. Despite this, when he asked for compensation for the loss of his money and his slaves, he was refused.

The new governor was a decent enough person but had a weakness for women and did exactly what pleased him in sexual matters. He created many embarrassing situations for himself at the fort but he did not care. Once out of prison, Fredericus found himself a Mulatto girlfriend who he happily shared with Dorph. Fredericus understood Dorph's limitations, but was glad to be back in the administration rather than in the 'Black Hole'. So he went on as he had in the past: assisting in the selling of slaves to the British, the Dutch, the French, the Spanish and the Portuguese traders who anchored their ships off the busy coast.

But this happy arrangement ended in February 1744. A new governor, Jurgen Billsen, arrived from Copenhagen to take over from Dorph, who had only held the post for eight months. Billsen found clear cases of embezzlement and theft at the fort. The incompetence of Dorph was so great that he was immediately put into detention. An order had also come from Copenhagen to remove Fredericus from all of his duties and to send him home. However, Pastor Meyer had become a drunkard, incapable of writing or transcribing from Latin, so Billsen temporarily needed the help of Fredericus until the next Copenhagen ship came.

The new governor Billsen, who came with his sister, tried very hard to organise the trading activities at the fort, which were in a complete mess, with new rules and regulations. Even though he had twelve domestic slaves himself, he tried to minimise corruption, criminality and theft, as the Company's warehouses were almost empty and profits were so poor. But almost all of the senior people at the fort were involved, one way or another, in criminal activities. Many of these profiteers, led by Sergeant Petersen, were naturally dissatisfied with the new strict measures.

After more criminal investigations, some of the high-ranking slave traders such as: Simon Klein, Romer, Hackenberg, the book-keeper Blass and Sergeant Petersen were sent to the "Black Hole" by the governor, where Petersen remained for sometime. Unfortunately for Billsen, all of these imprisonments triggered a mutiny by the fort's Danish soldiers and officials. After one Sunday evening church service, they gathered and drank so much schnapps that they were out of control and mutinied. The drunken mob appointed Klein, as he had been the longest at the fort, to confront Billsen and demand that he gave up his position. All this time Fredericus, who had been badly shaken by the cruel six months imprisonment, stood aside and watched the rebellion.

Governor Billsen, inevitably, was replaced by the rebellion's choice, Klein. The plan was that Klein was to be the interim governor until one came from Copenhagen to replace Billsen. Billsen was also ordered to leave the governor's suite of rooms. He protested and invited two respected traders from the Dutch and the British Forts, Mr Mijheer Kaymann and Mr Dithmar, to come and mediate. In a typical British compromise, the rebels agreed that Billsen should hold his title and stay at his residence, while Klein took over the day to day activities of the governor. In the end, all the top officials who had been sacked, including Romer and Blass, were reinstated with big bonuses, as were all the soldiers. But Sergeant Petersen was released from his cell much later on. An enquiry was held about the events of 1744 and Fredericus was the administrator who prepared all the official documents to be sent to the company's office in Copenhagen.

This was not the final upheaval at the fort. In March 1745, Billsen was suddenly taken ill suffering from one of the usual 'climatic fevers'. As the former governor did not trust his own surgeon, a Swedish doctor called Engmann, Fredericus was instructed to contact the surgeon at the Dutch Creveceur Fort to come and see him. Unfortunately, the surgeon turned out to be another drunkard who, worse, was a good friend of Billsen's arch enemy, Sergeant Petersen. To make matters worse still, Petersen's local wife from Osu village, whose Danish name was, Anna Sophie, had a father who was a medicine man (a witch doctor) at the village. Therefore every African and European at the fort believed that the drunken Dutch surgeon had overdosed Billsen, whilst the witch doctor had cursed him from the village. Billsen died very quickly with Fredericus at his side.

Former governor Billsen was buried the next day but a lot of the fort's officials who were offered the position as interim governor refused. One official, called Thomas Brock, who was foolish enough to accept the position, died suddenly after just twelve days. The next official appointed died one month later. The situation at the fort became critical. Finally, as none of the fort's officials would accept the governorship, the chief slave trader at Fredensborg Fort, named August Frederik Hackenberg, accepted the interim position. Unfortunately, Hackenberg spent all his time and energy buying and selling slaves for his own enrichment; so much so that the old problems of embezzlement, theft and drunkenness, quickly reappeared. This no longer mattered to Fredericus. He left Guinea Coast on the next ship with no baggage, no money, no proper clothes and not even knowing whether his wife Trina, his son Elias and his father Elias were still alive.

CHAPTER 17
REUNION

After ten years of working at Christiansborg Fort, and twelve years after he had landed on the coast, Fredericus's mission on the Guinea Coast had failed. In the autumn of 1746, he was put on board the *Williamina Galley* bound for Copenhagen. The ship sailed via St Thomas, in the West Indies, where the slaves were unloaded and sugar molasses were loaded for Copenhagen. The weather was kind to Fredericus for the home journey and he landed in Copenhagen in the spring of 1747. All the way from Africa, he speculated about the whereabouts of his wife and son after their eight years separation. He also thought about his father, Pastor Svane, as well as what he was going to do when he arrived in Copenhagen without any money to buy food and to pay for lodgings.

After Fredericus had landed, he walked to the middle of Copenhagen. He walked passed Christiansborg Castle, now renamed Christiansborg Parliament House. He also walked through most of the old familiar streets in the area, such as the Fiolstræde. He passed the university building, the Frue Kirke cathedral, the students' residence and, the Regensen, where he used to live. He wandered past all the familiar places in central Copenhagen. But he did not know what to do. After some time, Fredericus decided to go to the offices of the Company, The West Indian-Guinean Company, situated on the Knippelsbro near what was Christianborg Castle. He decided to go there to ask for help, to ask for employment and also to borrow a little money for food and accommodation for the night.

Standing at the front door of the Director's office, Fredericus took one deep breath and entered the room. To his astonishment the man, who was sitting at the desk, was a person he knew very well from the past. It was Duke Carl Adolph von Plessen. Von Plessen, who was nearly seventy years old, was dressed in formal clothes. The old man was surprised to see Fredericus and therefore, he received him warmly and, after offering Fredericus a cup of coffee, von Plessen asked him what he had been doing on the Guinea Coast since he left Denmark so hurriedly twelve years before.

Fredericus was only too happy to recount his story and poured out his woes to von Plessen. The old man found the story he was hearing very strange confusing and complicated. However, he advised Fredericus to go and write out a proper application for employment. To his delight, von Plessen told Fredericus that his wife and son were alive, as was his father; they were in good health and still lived at the Sorterup Vicarage. At the end of the meeting, the Duke even gave Fredericus some money for the few overnight stops at inns on the journey so he could be reunited with his family. Fredericus left the office in an extremely happy frame of mind. It took Fredericus a few days to walk to Sorterup where he was finally reunited with his wife Trina and his eleven-year old son Elias. His father, Pastor Elias, who had lost his first wife, had married Anna Cathrine Gregersdaughter, a daughter of another pastor.

As Fredericus had a great deal of psychological trauma, it took him one whole year to write his memoirs that covered the time he had arrived in Denmark as a schoolboy up to the day that he was repatriated from the Guinea Coast. The memoir was a plea for mercy. It was written in order that he might be pardoned and once again find employment in the Company. It described in detail his often chaotic life on the African coast. Fredericus's 'General Declaration' was delivered to the West Indian-Guinea Company in Copenhagen on the first day of June 1748.

CHAPTER 18
THE GENERAL DECLARATION

Fredericus wrote The General Declaration (1748) as a plea for mercy and help in order to be pardoned and gain re-employment in the The West Indian-Guinean Company's establishment in Copenhagen. The plea was addressed to the same old Director of the Company, Duke Carl A von Plessen. It was so important that Fredericus walked to Copenhagen to deliver it personally. After delivering the document to the office, he, Trina and their son returned to live with his father and stepmother at Sorterup Vicarage. Fredericus waited anxiously for a reply from von Plessen; sometimes losing patience he would again walk to Copenhagen, call at the offices of the company and enquire about its progress.

After waiting in total about nine months without hearing anything from von Plessen, Fredericus decided also to approach the Archbishop of Zealand, Bishop Peder Hersleb, and ask him for employment as a pastor. He argued that he would be capable of holding such an office because of his experience in Africa. Fredericus even offered to take the pastors' university examination to prove his capability. However, the Bishop refused to offer him such a position, partly because he remembered how Fredericus, as a member of the Pietist organisation, had condemned certain basic principles of the Lutheran Church's teachings on Christianity.

Finally, the bishop suggested to Fredericus that he might work under a pastor, as a parish clerk. However, King Frederik V, would have to issue a special decree to allow him to hold such an office. Clerks also had to teach in church schools but Fredericus had no teaching qualification. Fredericus argued, in a humble way, that he had been teaching Mulatto children on the Guinea Coast. The Bishop replied that teaching African children was not the same as teaching Danish children. However, His Majesty might, nevertheless, grant him dispensation to teach.

In the application to King Frederik V for a dispensation for Fredericus, Archbishop Hersleb summed up Fredericus's life story on the Guinea Coast: how he had served the Company for nearly eleven years, and how, since he had got back, he had been living in poverty with his wife and son without income. The reference from Hersleb clearly worked and King Frederik V signed a decree in favour of Fredericus.

The next thing Fredericus did was to return to the office of von Plessen who had also seen the King's decree. As a result von Plesson quickly promised Fredericus that if there became a vacancy for a parish clerk or a secretary on one of his manor farms, he would inform him without delay. Some months later, after Fredericus had again walked for a few days from Sorterup to Copenhagen, he arrived at the offices of The West Indian-Guinea Company. This time he received the good news that Lord Holberg, Professor at the University of Copenhagen, whom Fredericus knew from his university days, would have a job for him as a clerk and a teacher in a little parish called Havrebjerg. The village, which was part of a big estate belonging to the Barony of Terlosegaard, to which Holberg belonged, was situated just south west of Copenhagen.

Before he could gain the post, Fredericus had to write another application. This time he walked to the Terlosegaard estate and delivered his application to Holberg. Like the archbishop before him, Holberg recognised Fredericus as the young student who had been a member of the Pietist rebellion fifteen years earlier. Despite this, Holberg welcomed Fredericus warmly and offered him a warm cup of coffee while he read through the application. At the end of the application Fredericus had signed:

"*Fredericus Petri Svane Africanus*

via Catecetus et Cantor in Ecclellum Christiansborggum in Africa."

Holberg was amused by the application's interesting signature and title. He offered Fredericus a job immediately as the parish clerk at the village of Havrebjerg. Fredericus started working at the beginning of October 1749, two years after leaving Christiansborg Fort. As Bishop Hersleb had stated, he had to work under the parish pastor, a man called Gunther. Fredericus's duties meant that he had to also teach children in two other outlying village schools: at Blæsinge and Krænkerup. This was all rather fortunate, as Havrebjerg Parish was not far from his father's vicarage. There was great jubilation when he got back to his father's vicarage at Sorterup and told them the news. The post also meant that Fredericus was entitled to live in a little thatch roofed house with a large garden. In addition to this accommodation, as parish clerk he received some acres of agricultural land with some animals for provisions. For the school teaching, he was to be paid 12 *Rigsdaler* a year.

CHAPTER 19
THE PARISH CLERK AT HAVREBJERG VICARAGE

Fredericus, Trina and Elias were now looking forward to going to their new home. Pastor Svane and his wife were also going to be able to relax after having house guests for over nine years. However, problems would continue to dog Fredericus. The first school at Havrebjerg village was a very small whitewashed building with about fifty children of all ages cramped together in one classroom. The unwashed clothes, damp feet, smelling clothes and the lack of regular baths for these children made the smell in the classrooms unbearable. This was made worse in wintertime, when doors and windows were closed and smoke from wood burning in the fireplace also filled the room. Fredericus was used to warm weather and the fresh sea breeze on the Guinea Coast. Worse, educationally there were only a few copies of children's ABC books, arithmetic books and only a few copies of St. Luke's Christian Gospel. Fredericus also found it very hard to teach fifty children with only one tiny chalkboard.

The next problem was that, following a series of misunderstandings and disagreements, his teaching salary was reduced to 6 *Rigsdaler* a year and, even at this reduced rate, Fredericus found it difficult to get his salary paid by Lord Holberg. Therefore the family had to work very hard in the fields and also had to breed livestock in order to make ends meet. In addition to this hard farming life, and being the parish clerk, Fredericus also taught in the other schools.

The biggest problem, however, was that people in the three villages belonging to Havrebjerg Parish did not like Fredericus as he did not look like one of them. Pastor Gunther, his senior, was neither a nice person nor a good preacher of the gospels and he did not like

Fredericus much either. All these problems made Fredericus and his family very unhappy at Havrebjerg. Fredericus even referred the matter of his salary, unpaid for three years, to senior officials of the church in the district, but nothing happened.

Romer & Fredericus

Finally, Fredericus borrowed some smart gentleman's clothes and went to Copenhagen. There he contacted a few influential people and asked them to accompany him to an audience with King Frederik V to present his case. This visit to court caused much commotion. In Copenhagen the case involving Fredericus caused a split of opinion and some antagonism amongst the courtiers. In the end, Holberg wrote officially to Archbishop Hersleb that Fredericus was not fit for his job. As a result of this letter, Fredericus's complaint was dismissed. Unfortunately for Fredericus, Holberg died the following year without paying him. Fredericus even attended his funeral, with all the church dignitaries present, hoping that his four year salary arrears would be paid from the Holberg estate.

Gradually, the unhappy atmosphere in the family increased. Trina became more and more disappointed that she would never achieve the title of a pastor's wife. Elias, at the age of fifteen, was not at all interested in studying to become a Pastor like his father. Rather, he showed great interest in working with his hands. Thus Fredericus, disappointed that no-one would inherit his Latin and Greek books, reluctantly sent the boy as an apprentice to a local man who was a painter and joiner.

Fredericus, at this time, revived his old hobby of hunting and fishing to supplement their food supply. He borrowed a flintlock and used to wander the fields and forests around the parish hunting for hares, rabbits and pheasants. During one of his hunting trips, he stopped at the parish's cemetery to shoot at some birds making a mess. Unfortunately, there was a young local boy who had climbed a tree nearby to collect birds' eggs. When the boy heard the shooting, he got frightened, screamed very loudly and fell out of the tree to the ground. While he did not hurt himself, this episode caused rumours to spread around the district that Fredericus actually hated children and that he was possibly a potential child killer.

In another incident, as Fredericus was returning home, from a distant hunting trip with a friend, he put the hare that he had shot in his hunting bag. He was arrested near his home by the district game warden who locked Fredericus up in the dog kennels, accusing him of poaching. Even though he was innocent, Fredericus was so hated in the area that he could not explain himself and make the warden believe him. He was kept in the kennels for many hours until a hunting colleague, who had been with him earlier in the day, was contacted to confirm his innocence.

Gradually, the shaky relationship between Fredericus and Pastor Gunther also deteriorated. First, the old pastor became frightened of Fredericus when he walked about in the parish gardens with his flintlock dangling on his shoulder. Second, there was a strange episode in which someone, through negligence, left the keys of all the church's offices in one of the doors. Fredericus, being the parish clerk, was supposed to keep an eye on whatever went on in the church. He was also supposed to lock the doors of all the offices, including the attic room where the church weapons and ammunition were kept. After this incident, Fredericus guarded the keys so closely that he would not even leave open the cloakroom for the Pastor to get his ceremonial robes on for the performance of the Holy Communion the next Sunday. This incident led to an open quarrel between Pastor Gunther and Fredericus during the service itself. The embarrassed congregation left the church quickly and quietly.

In another episode, the young man who fell from the tree at the cemetery, physically attacked Fredericus, the Parish Clerk, during a church service. There was even fist fighting between the two of them in church. In another episode, it was reported that Fredericus, the teacher, had whipped some school children because the children had teased him and had made fun of him in class calling him "nigger", "Satan", "child killer" and calling his wife "Fatty Trina". Fredericus was also accused of misusing the name of King Frederik V despite the fact that the king had helped him to get his job.

Unfortunately, many negative rumours about Fredericus circulated all around the entire area, gradually becoming wilder and increasingly negative. In the end, the fathers of some of the children also got involved and there were incidents of fist fighting between Fredericus and some of the men in the neighbourhood. Unsurprisingly, Fredericus became ever more isolated and more and more confused about the purpose of his life in Denmark.

Later, at Christmas, Fredericus wrote two letters of apology; one to Pastor Gunther and the other to the district dean explaining why he had taken certain actions. The Pastor refused to accept his letters and instead sent them to the district office. Dean Reenberg did not accept the letters either and, in turn, forwarded them to Archbishop Hersleb in Copenhagen. After reading the letters, the Archbishop wrote back to the dean asking him to have patience with Fredericus as he was confused and could not fit easily into Danish society. Even though he showed signs of being a God-fearing man and praised God in all his writings, Fredericus was caught between his African obstinacy and his fantasies about being a European. Members of the parish council were told, by the bishop, that they should have patience with Fredericus and warn him about his unacceptable behaviour. They were asked to put some restrictions on him and prescribe what he could do and what he could not do in the future.

With these instructions, Dean Reenberg took action without delay. On the 26th of January 1756 he convened a district parish meeting. The council then approved a number of rules that Fredericus had to follow. For example, first he was asked to respect his senior, Pastor Gunther, and not to call him "his fellow servant of Christ". Second, he must not misuse the name of His Majesty King Frederik V. Third, he must not go about in the neighbourhood carrying his flintlock to hunt or to frighten his neighbours. Fourth he must leave the children who teased him alone. Finally, he must also return the keys for the church's offices to Pastor Gunther. These rules, for Fredericus to abide by, were written down for him to sign. He signed the document. On that day, the 26th day of January 1756, he was so depressed that he entered Havrebjerg church, which was situated only a few metres from his humble little cottage and, with a knife, gently and carefully carved his name deep into the parish clerk's wooden bench:

FREDERICUS PETRI SVANE AFRICANUS

Fredericus, however, did not abide by his hunting restrictions. As a lonely man, he continued his hunting and fishing journeys because he and his wife were so poor that they needed food. He still received no pay whatsoever for his teaching work. He was reported to his seniors several times for breach of orders but he continued. However, one day he received payment of 12 *Rigsdaler*, part of the amount of money that the late Professor Holberg had owed him, from the new owners of the estate. Unfortunately it was too late; Fredericus was too deep in debt. The amount was not enough to help them pay their debts nor to save the family from being declared bankrupt.

The *Theologian* Slave Trader

After living in this situation of isolation and disillusionment for some years, Fredericus told Trina that they had to leave Denmark and go back to his mother's country on the Guinea Coast. Therefore he visited Copenhagen to enquire about a possible job in Africa. While in Copenhagen, he heard that his old friend Romer had come back from the Guinea Coast and had started his own business. Fredericus contacted him immediately. After having a fine lunch, talking and eating together, Romer informed Fredericus that, in his late fifties, he was simply too old to go back to work on the Guinea Coast.

Fredericus made another attempt. He went to the offices of a Danish missionary sect in Copenhagen. They were trying hard to set up a mission at Osu, the village next to Christiansborg Fort where he was born. Unfortunately, the missionaries, who had been sent there, died like flies so their office in Copenhagen was not keen to send more people to their death. Aside from this, not only was Fredericus too old to go on such a mission, but he also had a very strange and unusual curriculum vitae. He also had a bad reputation on the Guinea Coast as well as a bad reputation in Denmark. As he did not have the financial means to travel back to Africa, he returned home to Havrebjerg more disillusioned, more depressed and more isolated than before.

At Havrebjerg, he continued his lonely hunting and fishing activities. Villagers still teased him and Trina if they were at their gate. Tragically his son died as a young man. Fredericus remained in his job for only a few more years. He was very unhappy and confused because he did not find it easy to be understood in 18th century Denmark. Most Danes did not know that there were other human beings with different coloured skin existing on another continent; Fredericus was the only African they would ever meet. This was because the Danish slave traders did not bring any of their slaves directly to the Danish-Norwegian Kingdom in the 18th century. Fredericus was therefore caught between, not only two different cultures, but also two completely isolated worlds.

Christiana Knudsen

CHAPTER 20
THE TRAGIC END OF FREDERICUS

Fredericus was asked to stop work before he became sixty years old. He moved to the tiny cottage in the village of Havrebjerg that was offered him. Unfortunately, his wife Trina died so he lived alone for many years, still being teased and hated by the local villagers. Most of the time, he occupied himself hunting and fishing. During these long and quiet trips, Fredericus must have looked back on his complicated life: his illiterate mother named Margrethe, the name given her by his soldier father Henrik Petersen, a daughter of a poor village farmer from the village of Teshi not far from Christiansborg Fort; Petersen, a farmer's son from southern Jutland, Denmark, who had died at the fort only a few years after his son's birth. Fredericus must also have looked back on how, at the age of ten, he became a child soldier, and later, a schoolboy at the fort; his adoption by Pastor Elias Svane; his first journey to Copenhagen; his baptism and he would wonder that King Frederik IV was his godfather. He may well have looked back on his schooling at Sorterup and Slagelse where he was often mobbed for being a "brown monkey"; his lonely university life in Copenhagen; and his involvement in the Pietist evangelical movement which cost him his final university examination certificate.

Also, he must have looked back upon his hurried marriage to Catharina Maria Badsch, the daughter of a German artisan immigrant, a marriage rejected by his father; how he had borrowed money to join a ship to the Guinea coast with Trina; how he had given up his dream of missionary work as a second Paul among the natives and how instead he himself had started to buy and sell slaves. He must also have reflected on his dream of building a mansion for his family, a move that had led to the accusation of his planning to overthrow the governor thus leading to his imprisonment in the

The *Theologian* Slave Trader

'Black Hole'; on his being bound in sharp iron chains for six months; on his release and how he had witnessed the mutiny at the fort. He must also have thought about King Frederik V who had helped him find employment, as well as his old sponsors Duke Adolph von Plessen, Baron Holberg and the Archbishop of Zaeland, Bishop Hersleb. Fredericus would also likely have looked back upon his endless troubles with Havrebjerg's Pastor Gunther, Dean Reenberg and the district church's members, among the influential elite in Copenhagen, who had caused him so many problems.

Even in retirement, tragedies would continue to follow Fredericus. After the deaths of his father, wife and son, Fredericus was declared bankrupt. Then one day the tiny house, that had been given to him for his retirement, burned down. The fire claimed the few academic books which he cherished so much, as well as the last handful of clothes he had left. At this time he had no relatives, no friends, no money and only the clothes he wore. Fredericus was so poor and confused and muddled about his life's situation, that he had to take refuge in the nearest beggars' home in Slagelse.

Fredericus in the Beggars' House

Gradually, his health began to fail him. He became blind, deaf and dumb. He also lost all his teeth and his sense of smell, as well as sensitivity in his body. He urinated and attended nature's call in his tattered clothes; defecating on his bare, sleeping mattress. Because of his lack of teeth, he was given only porridge to eat. When he was put on a bench to sit and eat his meal, he could not hold the spoon properly. So, as he lifted it towards his mouth, he spilt the porridge on his soiled, unwashed clothes. His dribbling mouth wide open, his hands shaking, no longer able to smell his own urine and vomit, Fredericus must have repeated several times in his mind:

ME UT AMAS AMA - LOVE ME AS YOU LOVE

Then on his last morning, just as he breathed his last breath, Fredericus could perhaps also have imagined the drumming at his funeral in Osu, on the Guinea Coast. Around the fire his people danced to the same melody that was sounded for the Queen Mother Nana Yaa Pokuaa, the royalty mistaken for a slave, who was sold at the Christiansborg Fort. The drums would most likely have been beating in his old Ga language:

PARISH CLERK & TEACHER

FREDERICUS PETRI SVANE AFRICANUS

1710 - 1789

WE SYMPATHISE WITH YOU

In the beggars' house, his body was very quickly wrapped and placed in a cheap wooden coffin, then dumped into a hurriedly dug grave on the fringes of the Slagelse Lutheran Church cemetery for beggars. Fredericus had a Danish burial that befitted a pauper: no gravestone, no name, no flowers and no ceremony.

PART II

Christiana Knudsen

FREDERICUS AUTOBIOGRAPHY
THE GENERAL DECLARATION

INTRODUCTION

The General Declaration, hand-written in Gothic style, was a plea for help and mercy in order to regain employment. It took Fredericus one whole year to pull himself together to write the manuscript. It took another year before he was offered employment as a clerk and teacher in the Havrebjerg Parish. Despite its limited success for the author, one significant achievement for this ten year autobiography is that, Fredericus, unwittingly, gave the modern world a rare opportunity to read about the barbaric life style of the Christian slave traders at Christiansborg Fort from the inside.

The translation methodology of *The General Declaration was* a unique process. First translated from Gothic script into Old Danish, it included establishing the meaning of Danish words and sentences that were written well over 300 years ago. Indeed, Danish was a rather different language in the 17th and 18th centuries. In these periods, many words were written and spoken that modern Danes no longer use or even know the meaning of. These words have been carefully researched. The research has been conducted in dictionaries of old Danish. Some words presented extra challenges as they were specific to the intermingling of languages in an area with African trading posts from a number of nations. Such words turned out to be combinations of Danish and English or German or French. Also, some words appeared to be spelling errors or just a version of a word that Fredericus Svane preferred. There was also to some extent a different word order and sentence structure to what is used in modern Danish. In any case, the language in Fredericus Svane's account reflects a lively contact between nationalities as well as the general development of any language over more than 300 years. Once the old language of Fredericus Svane's account had been translated into modern Danish, the content, tone and atmosphere of his writing were faithfully translated and recreated into the style of English that befits the way he expressed himself.

THE ORIGINAL MANUSCRIPT

A SHORT, TRUTHFUL
CLEAR, LUCID AND DETAILED
GENERAL DECLARATION
AND ACCOUNT
OF THE EVENTS OF TEN YEARS
AT THE FORTRESS
CHRISTIANSBORG AT ACRA ON THE COAST OF GUINEA
IN AFRICA

FOR
YOUR EXCELLENCY
YOUR HONOUR AND HIGHBORN, ETC
MASTER MR CARL A VON PLESSEN
SECRETARY FOR THE ROYAL CHARTERED
DANISH WEST INDIAN AND GUINEAN
COMPANY´S GRACIOUS ORDER
IN THE DEEPEST HUMBLENESS, COLLECTED
AND COMPOSED BY
YOUR EXCELLENCY´S
AND SUPREMELY LAWFUL BOARD´S
LOWEST AND MOST HUMBLE
SERVANT AND MOST CEASELESS
INTERCESSOR FOR GOD

FRIEDRIK P. SVANE
FORMERLY PARISH CLERK AND CATECHIST
COPENHAGEN
1ST JUNE
AD 1748

YOUR EXCELLENCY
HONOURABLE COUNT
MR CARL ADOLPH VON PLESSEN
SECRETARY
FOR THE ROYAL CHARTERED DANISH WEST INDIAN AND
GUINEAN COMPANY
ALL DIRECTORS
HIGH BORN AND HONOURABLE
NOBLE AND HONOURABLE
MERCIFUL MASTER

Amongst all of Your Excellency's care and providence I consider the following to be the happiest, namely, your praiseworthy zeal and upright determination and your scrupulous care towards the affairs of the highly lawful Danish Company in Guinea in Africa. It is not within my powers to comprehend Your Excellency's incomparable mercy towards I his lowest and most humble servant. May our Lord be forever praised and blessed that He has opened Your Excellency's heart to the virtue of mercy towards I, his most lost sheep. From all my heart I do present, most humbly, my circumstances regarding my journey from Copenhagen to the Coast of Guinea as well as my return here to the North. Moreover, with the greatest attention and humility I observe Your Excellency's most gracious order of 23rd April 1748 to put my request in writing, as follows:

The reason which forced me to leave Copenhagen to aim for the Coast of Guinea to apply there for keep and work in the service of the honourable company and my circumstances in this position and at that location, as well as the subsequent distressing and painful misfortunes, my graduation, the highest Almighty's miraculous providence, which happily has accompanied me to Copenhagen the seat of justice in the North, will subsequently be demonstrated in this most humble account.

[FREDERICUS WRITES ABOUT HIS LONELINESS AT UNIVERSITY]

In the Lord's year of 1734, when I was lodging at Regensen and enjoying the high royal maintenance at the royal university following the royal, most gracious privilege, in order to study for the exam in Theology and I was by the grace of our Lord capable of obtaining this, I was seized by a particular energy and enthusiasm to contact and engage in dialogue with a true and visible church of God. I came upon some people who were, in their outward appearance, conversation and discourse, strangely religious, about whom I thought in my simplicity that the church of God which in earlier times certainly was prevailing unfailingly, had to be found and be left later.

In the meantime, I engaged myself in this, to my firm belief to be true church of God. There occurred several attempts to discard the things, which in discourse, as well as in relations to others within this congregation of so-called Christians, were objectionable to this visible church, even if this should happen with some damage, persecution and scorn.

Amongst many other things that I strived to discard was the one about "Excercilio, Disputum de Quotidi*ano*" at the cloister where there were amongst other useful, though to my mind, at that point, useless and vain practices. Theology's even greatest and most holy secrets of the faith were practised and this sometimes by young and inexperienced students and this was not only with the disregard for the veneration appropriate for our Lord, but even with much appearing objection as one would have the advantage over the other when such high and holy matters according to my thoughts, just like before the face of God, should be accommodated with the very greatest respect.

These opinions I disclosed to my friends, who applauded me in this and approved my dispositions from which I became even more animated to make this firm resolution to implore myself for "Padres Academia" (our academic fathers or advisers), the then Professor of Theology, Steenbuck, now blissful in God's Heaven, and Professor Voldicke, whom I confess, did listen to these my fickle-minded thoughts with the greatest sympathy and sorrow and employed all imaginable and thorough reasons in order to get me away from self-created opinions, impressing on me that what I implored was merely misuse which had crept in, which could not, or should not, cancel out the right and true use and purpose of such "Academic Excercitier" such as the student youth's scrutiny regarding the healthy and true blessed knowledge, as well as Confirmation in the same way that a few dispirited minds between good and bad such as they, who should merely have a wise and firm intellect about and concerning the form of sound scholarship, but yet also in its peculiar way be powerful in refuting those who were opposing.

These fathers employed all possible efforts in order to get my unstable and fickle mind into a calm disposition in order to conform to these old academic statutes. And to these and several more diffuse persuasions from the very venerable fathers, I applied, according to my humble thoughts, my ideas about this, which they kindly approved and reformed, but when I on several occasions had had the honour and freedom of treating the subject with these venerable men besides having proposed my case to my then private tutor Mr Gram, Councillor of State, may He be blissful in God's Heaven, and not being able to come to any agreement with them but became rather consistent in my firmly preconceived scruples, the following happened: I, in accordance with the academic statutes, became excluded from the hall of residence, Regensen, and the cloister. Now, I was excluded from all human help; my circumstances were poor, I was fatherless and motherless in a foreign land and knew of no resort for a scanty stay.

Winter was approaching and, as the proverb goes, "Intet at braende og langt mindre at Bide" – "No fire to cook, and nothing to eat". I was without even the most basic means. Our Lord who saw my upright sincerity in this fickle-mindedness, my poverty and great need called upon the pious and compassionate heart of Mr Pipper, the then kitchen master at the Royal Orphanage "Det Kongelige Vajsenhus", who offered me his free board at lunch and dinner. May the Lord not let him or his seed want for bread. I perceived this offer as a peculiar ray of mercy from God and it was accepted with the greatest and most respectful thanks. I then took up lodgings with a poor craftsman in Fiolstraede, in the centre of Copenhagen, in trust of God's great and continued Providence which also displayed its rays and manifestations even more openly each day, as He guided my thoughts during these occurred conditions to Your Excellency, the most honourable master, Mr Adolph Carl von Plessen, who several times, even with his own merciful hands, saved me in the hours of need.

Put in one word: God's great Providence was indescribable. Him be praised as I survived over the winter. As winter was now over and I knew of no need, thanks to God's strange and special care for the outward daily needs, such as when I found in myself any considerable defects and limitations, I then took my refuge in God's unchanging and trustworthy retreat for everybody helpless and in need. Your Excellency Mr Carl Adolph von Plessen the Lord's beloved and faithful servant, God bless him and reward him with mercy, the Lord let his beautiful grey hair with his age and deeds remain alive for the time to come, that the desirable strength of his old age may be special and splendid just like the strength of his youth until he, after yet many days to the comfort and refreshment of many more destitute, eventually shall be claimed on "Elias'" carriage and be moved from here to the God of "Elias" and his God, and, for eternity be entertained in the most delightful view of the Lord's most blessed face, and then harvest the most glorious fruits of his long labour, when His Excellency who, here, has been without children can bring hundreds of children before God's face, saying: Lord, look, here am I and the children whom you have given me. And how often this man of God, a father to many children in need, has refreshed my heart in my need and want, God knows best.

[FREDERICUS FINDS REFUGE WITH THE PIETISTS]

In the meantime, I conversed with no other than the good friends, who were people that had separated themselves from the congregation of the large common church, the so-called Christians, and were therefore, as is known, called Separatists. With the greatest pleasure I realised, now and then, that even this, after my wise and strong opinion about it, God's true and visible church, had many shortcomings, when one considers it and compares it with the Church of God at the time of the Apostles. Then I consider myself somewhat deceived in my thoughts as there begins to be almost as many opinions as there are heads and serious internal division and disagreement. I now found myself in such a state of doubt in, according to my thoughts, the imaginary God's true and visible church in which, I had assured myself of an Angelic being and life on Earth. Yet, having been so badly deceived, my thoughts then became quite changed, albeit with much uneasiness and many concerns on my poor mind. God shall be my witness.

I knew no way out as to where I should turn my unstable mind in order to obtain any kind of purity. I was in this disquieting state of mind that I saw no human being to whom I could have any benefit in confiding my bad and difficult destiny, who was of any significance, on whom to base my eternal calm. My condition was all the more dangerous, as it appeared to me amongst other peculiar concerns of taking holy communion at the altar with a stab of conscience together with the large external congregation of God's church consisting of known and unknown, evil and good, people. I had fallen into such circumstances by being in company of the aforementioned good, upright and imaginary Christians, so my last distress was greater than the first.

[FREDERICUS DECIDES TO LEAVE DENMARK]

My mind was now completely troubled; all hope was in vain, so I almost perished. Still, the merciful God who has always helped in the hour of need turned my thoughts away from this, so that I firmly decided to seek calm in the least calm land in the world, by which I mean my native country at the Coast of Guinea, called Accra as now, I thought that nowhere in the world was there a visible God's church anymore. At the emergence of these new thoughts, my own troubled mind gained some kind of solace. God knows where from! Because I thought in my then blindness and happiness, darkness of ignorance, that I could more easily, by God's grace teaching in silence, be able to summarize for myself, considering and investigating these important things even more so in this land, and blindest heathenism was not to be feared for obstinate opinions in the orthodoxy since they who have no religion have no reason which is hidden and unknown to them nor unknown to us and therefore, these lands revealed and proclaimed the most precious treasure in God's blessed teaching.

In addition, I got the firm hope by the condition of God's blessed mercy to reach the aim and purpose of my few studies as well as that of the honourable directors and my reverend father, Mr Elias Svane, whose good intentions were also working for me: namely, the perpetual blessing of the Lord for me to undertake the conversion of the heathens in my dear native land on the Coast of Guinea, so that I follow the admonition of the Saviour to help my people, as said by the Evangelists:

> "WHEN YOU HAVE BEEN CONVERTED, THEN STRENGTHEN YOUR BRETHREN"

I could now achieve my purpose in my prayers to God that he could equip my unworthy person's spirit and power from High, so that my arrival to the heathens in Africa could be so blessed by the Lord just like my association with them; that I with my humble talent as a faithful servant could work although under voluntary confession of great flaws and numerous weaknesses. I confess before the face of the Lord, that I was so delighted about these lovely notions, about the firm hope for the converting of heathens in Africa, that I by the spirit of the Lord, which appeared so powerful in my weakness, hoped to work miracles in Africa. Yes, God be my witness, I was still thinking of becoming the second "Paul" in the world. So grand were my preconceived imaginations about these delightful, blessed hopes.

Because of this wonderful state of mind, in which I found myself, about carrying out the blessed Service, in Africa, 1 more or less ignored my previous destructive worries and scruples. Thus, the present, heavenly joy, to some extent, overrode my previously mentioned serious worries. But as no joy is so sweet that it cannot, nevertheless be added an unexpectedly hideous bitterness, so was also this present great joy not without wants as new worries appeared.

All my thoughts went to the Coast of Guinea in order to come away from the great disquiet in the religion that existed even amongst the good people with whom I had been conversing so confidently during the entire winter. Amongst them were almost, as the proverb has it; "as many heads as there are minds". There was a tough nut for me to crack about how I could get to the coast. I had no gold or silver with which to pay for my freight, transport and food.

The gracious gentlemen, the Directors, had hitherto from my youth and owing to my Reverend father Mr Elias Svane's upright diligence, spent considerable costs on my education, not only in my schooling as a child during my elementary instructions, but even kept me studying later on in a private school in this country, which was supervised by my father Mr Elias Svane under the discipline of my school master, the much beloved and highly learned candidate Mr Nicolaj Ovesen Guldberg, the minister of the Word in Naestved and later on, also here at the royal university, until I, from absolute royal grace, enjoyed the cloister and the hall of residence , Regensen. I did not dare to ask for free transport to the coast as I knew full well, that the gracious masters' previously great favour towards me had to a great extent cooled off by my earlier behaviour being, that I had made acquaintance with Pietists (Evangelicals and Separatists) here in this city and had been conversing with these contrary to the masters' wishes and serious admonitions given to me and just for the sake of keeping this company with these peculiar people and with fantasy, I had lost the absolute most gracious royal scholarship wherefore the gracious masters did not have the previous willingness and great fondness towards I, their very highly obliged and most humble servant.

[FREDERICUS'S MARRIAGE AND JOURNEY TO THE GUINEA COAST]

Necessarily, I needed money to pay for my food and transport to the coast and besides this concern, another one of equal significance had arisen. This was so, as I found myself in a doubly important situation namely, that some time before I had become engaged to, not unintentionally but in deliberation with God, a good-natured and respectable woman here in this country in the town where I had attended school. This was Catharina Maria Badsch, the daughter of a joiner, though I confess that my reverend father Mr Elias Svane who was extremely against this, possibly had another opinion concerning my welfare in this my most important venture, my earthly and as good as eternal welfare so greatly regarding this. Yet I went my own way under God's reliable guidance, so well knowing the importance of marriage and the Highest divine condition in my important venture, with which my honourable and most reverend father was not pleased and therefore set up several obstacles for us. But all circumstantialities aside, the pious God drove, by Your Excellency, his chosen tool Mr Carl Adolph von Plessen, who removed these obstacles out of the way and carried out his purpose with me his servant just like He, the good Lord, has since ceaselessly shown his peculiar care of me in a miraculous way during all events, to put it shortly,

"The Lord's name be praised".

I got my wife, was and am pleased with her, and the payment for her transport should also be seen as part of my debt, which had reasonably been demanded. However, as the following shows, the Lord took all grief from me and cared fatherly for both of us. Under these difficult circumstances, I immediately decided to take refuge with Your Excellency, honourable master, Mr Carl Adolph von Plessen whom the Lord roused to see to mine and my companion's planned transport and journey to the coast where after the events took place as follows: I paid my usual, most humbly respects at Your Excellency's previous gracious permission to let me submit my petition to your high court concerning my most humble matter which was, at this time, that I had resolved to travel to the Coast of Guinea in Africa, my dear native land.

This my conceived decision, Your Excellency, my gracious Master, assented to and certainly most graciously approved of with the query of the peculiar mercy, if not I would take up a position in the country be it secular or ecclesiastical, then I should get. Whereupon, I made my most duly and humble compliments for promotion and commitment on the pretext of the poor condition there on the coast of the service of the fortress and the company, of which I knew very well and of which I had heard sighs and hints every day from my right honourable father, Mr Elias Svane. I had my own knowledge of these hardships, as in my early youth I had experienced these too, owing to the unlawful administration by the president of the court and other dangerous circumstances, which caused the greatest inconvenience to respectable and God-fearing minds.

Out of fear for such already known danger and harm, persecution and pursuit over there, I made my most humble excuse for not taking up any position in the service of the most lawful Company there, but would travel there as a missionary under the care and Providence of our Lord, for the conversion of the heathens, which Your Excellency did not particularly approve of but left it to my own free will.

Nevertheless, Your Excellency paid our journey and transport but did order me to offer to pay for this myself. Upon Your Excellency's mildest attention and care for me, I embarked on my journey to the countryside in order to celebrate the wedding to my fiancée sweetheart and wife, with much circumstantiality which, for the sake of brevity, shall be passed over in silence, eventually reached its consummation.

But when I then arrived back in Copenhagen and the ship was ready for sea as favourable winds were expected, I discovered that Your Excellency was not in town but had travelled off to the countryside and this unexpectedly arisen situation left me somewhat dismayed in my plans. But what could be done about it? The fastest decision was then the best. I made a memorandum book for the most lawful, highly respectable board regarding transport for my wife and I to the Coast of Guinea with the attached most humble notice regarding Your Excellency's most gracious promise to pay for us but that I should, though, offer the board to pay myself whereupon I, your most humble servant, obtained from the Bookkeeper, Monsieur Mariager, the high board's favourable decision and bill for 8 Danish Marks per person, namely 2 Rigsdaler and 4 Marks per week for myself and my wife, to be paid and should be paid as soon as possible, when God permitting, on my arrival at the Coast.

[FREDERICUS AND WIFE ARRIVE ON THE GUINEA COAST, 3rd AUGUST, 1735]

Upon this, and in the name of Jesus under the Almighty's merciful Providence and presence, my spouse and I embarked in all our lowly poverty on our journey to the Coast of Guinea, for Christiansborg, onboard the ship named "JOMFRUEN" (The Virgin), in the Lord's year of 1735 and spent 12 weeks completing the journey. We arrived at Christiansborg in Guinea Coast, happy and well in the name of the Lord in the month of August, three months after our departure from Copenhagen, God be forever praised. I took up lodgings for myself and my wife with one of my former school friends called Severin, according to the agreement made with him the previous year in Copenhagen. This good and faithful school friend showed us no small but all imaginable service, honesty and politeness. He was living in a recently built two-storey house.

He allocated to us the rooms on the top floor and took the rooms on the ground floor for himself so, in this respect, we were met with all the comfort we could possibly want. On my arrival, I immediately encountered this hard and serious ordeal and renunciation regarding my trust in the Lord and his divine Providence, namely the board's honourable new governor of the fortress and the coast, counsellor Mr Schielderup who had been travelling with us. He submitted quite a strict order regarding me and my wife's transport on the ship and board on the journey with the following content, that His Honour was immediately on our arrival under orders to command me to pay for our transport and aforementioned board, which, in Copenhagen, by the board, was agreed and pledged to be of the cabin's food on board the ship, although not supplied by the captain but with ignorance concerning this by the board. Furthermore, the Governor was warned to be very careful not to take me into the service of the Company as I was a heretic, who could possibly seduce all the staff of the company there.

Mr Schielderup did have other positive thoughts on this matter having been with us on the out- bound journey and on our further lawful life and conditions in Copenhagen. Although His Honour would very much like to help, yet he did not dare to breach the strict and express order from the Honourable Gentlemen on the Board of Directors, which many people there were well aware of; that as soon as I had arrived in the country I had to clear the bill which had been given to us regarding our transport and board: this still outstanding bill. This I could not meet, as I was, in the first instance, hindered by our lowly poverty. In accordance with my own offer, I therefore accepted, for the time being, to give away my black, good as new, tailored suit along with two other suits that I acquired some time ago in Copenhagen from Your Excellency and which, I had indeed worn in the same town, too. The above mentioned black suit of mine I received again a short time before I took up my post, as it was returned to me from His Honour against a reduced entry in my salary book, which amounted to the sum of 32 Rigsdaler.

Finally, I found my dear mother, siblings, brothers, and several others of my relatives and family on my mother's side in a rather bad and miserable condition, which was contrary to the hopes I had in Copenhagen. So although they were one of the most distinguished families in the area, their circumstances were yet so bad, on the whole, that they needed my help more than they were able to help me in even the most modest way with the necessaries of life and, in this respect, it was the case with us that we did not own any Rigsdaler. However, the Lord who had not at any point, in any need and want, rejected me but who had always shown his fatherly care towards me in my toilsome life, nor did He leave me in this similarly present deficiency and lack of the daily necessaries of life. As his divine Majesty had supplied and provided me with a faithful and dear, honest companion, He now let me, the good Lord's most humble servant though full of flaws and much weakness, see the first good examples of his deepest care towards I, in that country. This was the sincerity of my honest wife's genuine, sincere and loving friendship and diligent industry, which was blessed by the Lord.

My dear wife's parents, whose faithfulness and genuine affection the Lord will reward, had brought up their daughter not for idleness and laziness but for labour and diligence, so she was not used to unemployment but had always been interested in having work to do and to earn something with her own hands, to the benefit of both of us. Therefore, she right away took up work when she realised, that I would not be able to earn anything in order to provide for her. So she agreed to sew for people on the Fortress, thereby earning the keep for her and I, until we could see and feel the pious God's further Providence and care for us for the future. So under the circumstances that had arisen, I had occasion to praise the Almighty's wonderful management of me and could therefore, in a sense, be free of remorse as I confess that my circumstances seemed very difficult to me.

[FREDERICUS EMBARRASSED AS PREGNANT CATHARINA CONTINUED TO WORK]

In the beginning, I found it hard to adjust to the circumstances. At the start of my marriage I had to find, that my fate was so meagre and my disadvantages so great that I, who ought to be supporting my wife, had to be supported by her. Yet she, for her part, should also adjust herself to this situation considering my situation without position and favour and to her marital duty as my helper, requested by God. It did not take long to find the strength and the opportunity to find work and earn an income. Thanks to no possible illnesses and frailties, she could work and at the same time be made pregnant, whereby these could go together. Therefore, in addition to her hard physical work, which could have either quite weakened her or taken from her the baby, God's grace granted and endowed her with strength. Both she and I, and the expected child or foetus, were in the greatest need for life's necessary maintenance, which we also, to a great extent, had to provide. But blessed be the Lord, who under so many different troubles and tribulations from adversity and worries has always let me survive, his most unworthy servant. Indeed, in addition to my sincere and lovable spouse, we saw new examples of his help as He displayed his fatherly care towards us.

In the meantime, I too was not entirely aimless either. I was occupied, though not with my hands, yet with the mind's perpetual worries and unceasing prayers and intercessions to God that His Divine Majesty with his fatherly Providence would, henceforth as well as hitherto, continue to be with us, and not to let us be utterly shamed in this our great want and complications, which were so grave and troublesome to us.

The Lord heard my weeping and received my sighs and allocated us daily as much necessary bread as we needed. He accommodated his fatherly care for us according to our capacity to receive them from him allotted part and need for us; yes, thus directed his fatherly care according to each of our occurred circumstances.

[FREDERICUS GIVES UP HIS DREAM OF MISSION WORK AND APPLIES FOR EMPLOYMENT AT CHRISTIANSBORG FORT]

In the meantime, I considered my condition to be very difficult and bad in relation to life's necessaries for my wife and for myself for the future. My firm hope about the common conversion of the heathens in Guinea by the assistance of God's spirit and my humble service began not only to diminish but also to die. There were not at all any apparent or presumed signs of this to be seen and experienced as yet because of the inherently difficult expressions in the country's language concerning the construction of religion's true and blessed foundations. Most important and profound truths about blessedness, such as the work of Christ the Redeemer, about the Holy Spirit and His presence within His children, His enlightenment, attendance and so on, could not be made clear in this language without the use of words, which were profane and inappropriate for the explanation of such holy matters. Then, I began thinking about applying for some kind of work in the service of the most lawful company. Upon this, I first applied verbally to Counsellor Mr Schielderup, the Governor, as he was a blessed memory.

I then saw the Honourable Mr Schielderup's kindness towards me. With great compassion, he put forward my humble and abject request and application and pledged to help me in the ways he was able to since he, according to my hitherto behaviour, could say or know of nothing evil or unsuitable, though he had added:

"You are somewhat out of favour with the Directors".

However, he could not yet give me any certainty before the return of the ship, which had transported us to Africa which due to the company's affairs "in negotia" was staggered along the coast and was expected in March or April, in the coming year. For this long, he

The *Theologian* Slave Trader

asked me to have patience and this was the situation for the time being. When the ship, thanks to God, arrived safely and happily at the above mentioned time, namely the 2nd of April in the year 1736 at the fortress, I as soon as possible submitted my previously mentioned matter to the Honourable Governor, Counsellor Schielderup and the Board at the same place at Christiansborg Fortress. I put this in writing, in its original form, the wording was the following, as here in *"sub litra B; ....."* (the application was not given in this autobiography).

By God's Providence and on the recommendation of the Honourable Mr Schielderup's kindness and the Reverend Erik Trane, Minister of the word here, that I was accepted into service of the respectable company, this happened without any previous agreement regarding years of service, neither how long or how short, how few or how many years. Though in my thoughts, not so many years, since I was thinking as soon as possible of trying again my luck in Denmark, if and when this would please the Holy God as well as please the honourable gentlemen company directors. It was, God knows, far from my thoughts before the application for service; I did not want to spend so many years, and the best years of my life in particular, in such poor and miserable ways as was possible at all, under the sun.

In the most humble account of this employment from when I first began in my position, I announced that I, in relation to the position of catechist and school teacher, certainly came across an only mediocre condition as I found before me not more than 6 to 7 children to teach. In addition, they had, following the existing lack of structure, no proper and decent education because, for some years now, the long standing arrangement made by my Honourable father Mr Elias Svane's god-fearing care, and the Honourable Gracious Gentlemen Directors' mildest and decent provision, had now been absolutely done away with.

I was told this was done by the former Governor Andreas Waeroe's unholy first administration and stinginess which had converted funds from the Honourable Directors for the use of the youths' decent upbringing, granted in part for keep and clothing, over to his own use instead. Therefore, the youths had got into such a bad condition that, worst and miserably of all, they had hardly, not to put too fine a point on it, any patches of clothes with which to cover themselves, let alone something to eat. Therefore, they could not really attend to their education, but each of them had to do as best they could by doing odd jobs for the soldiers or other functionaries at the Fortress in order to get their life's necessities.

This caused serious harm to the advancement of Christianity for the youths in the service of the company. This is so, as during all the time I have been in this position, I have not been able to make any optimistic, considerable progress and advance with them for any particular, advantageous outcome and use. I here know and confess to God and the Honourable Gentlemen that I, for this reason, with the most severe tediousness have been working in this position for many years serving the company, namely from middle of April 1736 till the middle of August 1746, which is 10 years. What I have endured in the meantime in this position as Parish Clerk and Teacher, and how miserable my life has been to me, God knows best, and how miserable and meagre my fate has been in all my time during this service owing to the trials and tribulations by the Provincial Administration, some due to hate and persecution, some out of envy and jealousy of my happiness granted to me by God.

In accordance with the content of Your Excellency's most graciously issued order to me, I shall describe truthfully the true condition of the matter as carefully and clearly, as brief and most necessary, and present the investigation to Your Excellency as if before God's face, who knows my heart and for whose all seeing countenance I imagine to present myself on that last day.

[FREDERICUS WRITES ABOUT GOVERNOR SCHIELDERUP]

Regarding His Honour Mr Schielderup, Governor and Colony Manager, his life, living and death as well as the administration during his time at the start of my position, with respect to the administration and the Governor in particular, Counselor Schielderup, Governor and Colony Manager: in this person, I found a brave man for a Governor who was sent by the Board in Copenhagen, together with us, in order to take over from the previous Governor, the Honourable Andreas Waeroe. The here mentioned blessed man, Mr Schielderup, I acknowledge, was such a brave man that his name and year will stand for as long as Accra exists on the Guinea Coast.

Immediately on his arrival and on meeting with the Administration, he began to create a wonderful hope about his blissful regime due to the strangely radiant light which went out from him concerning virtue, devoutness and upright zeal for the most lawful company and pious care and concern for the common good in the service of the company from the highest ranking to the lowest ranking. This was in his heart and it was a clear sign of his God-fearing nature. First and foremost, he brought changes to order he found at Fortress Christiansborg by the abolition of the hitherto odious practices and the organization of everything according to Christian order and tradition both of which to real advantage and use for the company as well as the common good of all the functionaries. This was a proof and a display of true Christianity and, in this case in particular, by the abolition of the black, heathen women at the Fortress; to restrain and subdue loose living and prostitution as well as drunkenness and gluttony; to keep good manners and discipline; to administrate fairness and justice; to lead a Christian life living amongst all the functionaries.

This Christian and blessed arrangement and reformation could not do anything but go with God's blessing which was also clearly evident throughout his time. He made trade flourish to such an extent and wealth to such a degree both on land and at sea that, according to everybody's accounts during his time, there was such a daily and continual trading as never seen before. So, in all he did, there was nothing but the Lord's pure blessing.

However, the lifetime of His Honour was unfortunately so very short, namely from only the 12th of August 1735 till the 20th of June 1736. Thus His Honour governed for 10 months and 8 days. Such end of which caused the most serious harm to the company and unceasing lamentation of the entire land and Fortress amongst blacks and whites.

[FREDERICUS WRITES ABOUT GOVERNOR ENEVOLD NIELSEN BORIS]

The Honourable Enevold Nielsen Boris, Governor and Colony Manager, started in the position as Governor. The following is an account of his administration and death:

Following the said Honourable Councillor Schielderup, the successor was Enevold Nielsen Boris, the previous Bookkeeper and Secretary, the second voice in the Secret Privy council, who also according to rank and order, was next in line to this position. However, according to the Board's instruction, it was in fact not necessary to comply with such an absolute as the elections for the Administration were not obliged to be carried out in accordance with the rank and the votes of the Secret Privy Council anyway, when this election was not preceded by prayer and God's supplication out of the Council, also where a gentle and God-fearing person is promoted for this post.

He began his rule with sobriety and justice, zeal and sincerity, in as much as one could sense and judge on the outside. With respect to his outward presentation, he appeared to be an honourable and gentle person, sober and modest for the world to see yet, as for the nature of his heart, known only by God, who alone knows the hearts of human beings, he was not what he appeared to be.

With respect to the company's trade, he acted as a sensible chap, faithful and honest, as far as I was aware, as he was attending to his business not merely as a good Governor but also as an appropriate bookkeeper. He had neither an assistant bookkeeper nor anybody else for this position during his time. God knows for what reason he was promoting this and moreover, why the honourable Mr Boris thus administered the position of three people himself. All of which not only I but even all the functionaries in the company at this time witnessed and I assumed that the books and documents he was keeping in the company's office though containing inanimate letters, bore living testimony after his death.

He treated all functionaries according to order and rank in an honourable and honest way and polite, so they were well pleased with him. Good discipline and a reasonably passable judicial system and administration were important to him. Still, with respects to I, and my dear wife, he conducted himself in such a manner that we cannot, with a good conscience, give him reference as being honest and respectable. He, who on our initial arrival had behaved very politely towards us, would later on let himself be impelled by the bad impulses of the flesh to demand indecent services and disgraceful favours from my wife.

She was the aim of his carnal, rude and impure lust which he could not attain, upon which he conceived schemes by all imaginable means and plots in order to retaliate against her continual rejections of his improper, dishonest, not to say, indecent quenching of lust, which was also the most truthful reason for our long parting as he was a highly placed figure whose authority, power and injustice I could not withstand in the defence of my wife.

With the foreign European nations present on the Coast, both on land and at sea, he kept a close and good relationship and friendship in the beginning, but as time went on he began to be on edge with the Dutch nation. However, prior to his death, this misunderstanding was settled at last.

As regards the end and death of the honourable Governor Boris, this came to pass as follows: prior to his death and departure, he had scheduled a journey to the Fortress Fredensborg in order to make enquiries from the then merchant Monsieur Nicolaj Jurgensen, who had thought of undertaking official duties in the same place and Fortress, Christiansborg. This was a rumour as well as a report which had come through to him, Boris, from his officials, concerning dealings with notorious and forbidden goods, to undermine the authority of his high position and awarded judgment. However, the fast and unexpected aggressive fever and dysentery set back this planned and approaching journey to Fredensborg Fortress at Ningo. Instead, the rapid approach of another journey and direction out of this world, as regards the way of all flesh, caused his most peculiar quick death and departure from the world. The duration of his administration and rule was four years in total: namely from the 20th of June 1736 until the 20th June of 1740, which was somewhat notable.

[FREDERICUS WRITES ABOUT THE PASTOR IN CHARGE OF THE FORT]

Next follows the first part of my time in the benefice at Christiansborg Fortress. Honourable and Learned, Mr Eric Trane during whose time I accepted the position of Catechist at the Fortress Christiansborg, regarding this very clergyman I must in truth confess that, upon my initial arrival to the Coast of Guinea, I was met by an absolutely compassionate heart, so too by his dear wife, now blessed Madam Helena Trane. When these good people first saw us in the country in such difficult circumstances without any favour and with wants and shortages of even life's necessary keep and my wife expecting a child even so one predicament for us was followed by the next, wherefore nothing more likely than great predicaments could be predicted for us, they offered to help us.

In his peculiar caring favour and good kind heart this man displayed an obvious sign of friendship from the start as he proposed a condition of the following nature: that the living and present clergymen in the service of the company on the Coast should have their salary separated from certain expenses for the education of their children and, in this way, according to his opinion, the teaching post should be separated from the position of the Catechist so that I, by this arrangement, could be promoted to the former and the Catechist alone could administrate the position and the service of the Catechist. However, after close scrutiny and consideration, this was something which he himself had to confess was not workable.

During his life, living and doctrine, he proved to be a true sincere clergyman when I first knew him; very zealous concerning honour and fear of God, as well as the abolition of ungodliness and the giving of perpetual admonitions to lead a life of virtue and sanctity, although, after the departure of his blessed wife in July of 1737, he became somewhat disturbed in his mind possibly owing to this blow and the concerns brought about by this genuine parting. During the entire time we were attached to the church service, a continuing friendship existed between us until his replacement and subsequent departure from the coast which took place in the middle of April in 1738.

The *Theologian* Slave Trader

[FREDERICUS WRITES ABOUT GOVERNOR PEDER JURGENSEN]

My, on his demands, given and now necessary testimonial has the following content and original: Honourable Peder Nicolaj Jurgensen, his promotion into the Administration, his rule, commencement, progress and eventual resignation from his high office.

After Boris's rapid departure from the world and from the Administration, into this vacant high office came a kind noble Peder Nicolaj Jurgensen, formerly a merchant and commander at the recently built Fredensborg Fortress at Ningo situated about 7.5 Danish miles, about 64 km from Christiansborg.

By nature this man possessed, not only a very soft effeminate heart, but also a yielding and susceptible disposition. This soft temperament of his led to, and also created, on his commencement in the governing position, only a poor hope for a happy and sensible rule, which the following incident without any doubt, on the day when he was elected and took up his position in the local Government as a Governor, clearly shows.

On this day, the current police Constable, Sergeant and Commander, namely Cornelius Pedersen, the then police officer in the service of the company, made for himself a cheerful and jolly day which was spurred on by his rude and disturbed mind. When he was now amusing himself according to his own opinion he went deliberately, and on purpose, straight to the recently laid out and beautifully blooming garden of the former Governor and, being in the power of his own drive, he felled all the lovely fruit trees in the said garden where after he turned up at the Fortress again. With cheerful and entertaining gesticulations, he delivered his account and made a show of this, according to his malicious personality, amusing acts and expedition. He said he had felled all the trees in the garden of former Governor Boris; since Boris was dead now, he saw nobody whom he regarded as worthy either of the garden itself or of the trees in it. He continued that as they were now without a master and owner other than himself, who had planted them, this had been done according to orders and commendation from the departed Governor

Boris, who with the police Constable's supervision of slaves' work had arranged this said garden not merely for himself but also for the pleasure and entertainment of the following and succeeding Governors.

What happened next? This was brought before the new Governor Jurgensen who asked the said Cornelius what this was supposed to mean. Yet, Cornelius, besides his many many possessive and imperious misdeeds, was also a big and boorish person who, so to speak, did not respect either God or any human being. He answered proudly, in the presence of a great crowd and stir of people at the Fortress, blacks as well as whites. He claimed that he had himself planted this garden for the pleasure and recreation of Boris, whom he considered worthy thereof, but as he was now dead and the garden now had no master, therefore, he had done what he had done for his own pleasure. In addition, at the same time, this vicious person was very noisy and alarming in the Fortress.

The recently elected and accepted Governor Jurgensen listened to the rudeness of this massive and immoral person with such softness and patience, that everyone who publicly attended, with the greatest amazement approaching indignation, predicted immediately from this poor beginning an only mediocre administration by and under Jurgensen. His subsequent, very unwise and foolish conditions and undertakings, certainly regarding my person, clearly and obviously showed this to be the case. This Governor Jurgensen was probably a good person; in fact, too good as, from his entire temper, one could not ascribe anything choleric to him. However, he was such a compliant and very kind person, according to his own imagined wisdom and fear of God, on the other hand, he was so very unwise and inconsiderate to let himself be ruled and ordered about, I believe, by even the smallest and most foolish of children. Nothing in his entire life was constant or fair or sensible so without doing him any injustice, one can only, with some good reason and fairness, give him a reference as being a respectable person.

Governor Jurgensen was probably kind-hearted and helpful towards everybody. He did nothing evil, when he could decide for himself, but did everything good towards everybody. Yet this, even according to my humble thoughts all of this, was not sufficient to call him a good person or even a wise and sensible Governor at Christiansborg Fortress. It would have been preferable that he had never been promoted to this dignified position. As he was a very helpful and charitable person towards everybody, this man and Governor certainly showed his great kindness and favour for and towards me. He did like to have me around for company and discussions, sometimes ecclesiastical and sometimes secular, all depending on how the whims of his unstable mood were.

I confess that he listened to my opinions and reasoning with a particular delight and pleasure but this was nevertheless so very flighty and inconstant. In truth, I have to say this about his great courtesy and particular favour towards me: that he sooner and continuously wanted me in his company than I wished to flatter myself or appreciated to be with him, although I had to, whenever or as often as he demanded, be it night or day, evening or morning, early or late, though sometimes very much against my will. This was rated, by nearly all the functionaries, as a particular advantage and luck for me. However this evoked much envy towards me. I would much have preferred that Governor Jurgensen had been less favourable towards me. How little advantage and use this special attention from Mr Jurgensen hereafter, distinctly and truthfully, be clearly demonstrated. I would not say with my conscience as a witness, that he, with any kind of good reason, could be denied these few lines about him and his circumstances.

I hope Your Excellency and all the Honourable Gentlemen can amplify the true connection of this case and the Administration during his entire period as Governor without anything more verbose than is necessary in order to present a short account. Therefore, I will pass over many of his whims and fantastic ideas, bad arrogance, inconstant eagerness for something or other, fuss and numerous strange and grimacing undertakings in his life and living, in relations and conversations even with the foreign nationalities about which could be told a story of a considerable verbosity and length. Yet this must be enough about the life and rule generally conducted by him with respect to my person in particular, the said Governor behaved and conducted himself very strangely and soon beyond comprehension. This is imparted most humbly to, and for, Your Excellency and Honourable most Gracious Gentlemen Directors.

[FREDERICUS VISITS FREDENSBORG FORT]

While I was carrying out my duties on the Coast of Guinea in Africa, at Christiansborg Fortress at Osu in Accra, as a Parish Clerk and Catechist, I undertook four journeys to Fredensborg Fortress at Ningo. Three journeys were pleasure and recreation journeys with exercise for the body and refreshment for the mind, which often was weakened and troubled due to several sometimes strangely hard and touchy incidents and difficult situations. These journeys to Ningo happened once with Mr Jurgensen and twice with Christen Glob Dorph, for both of them were, during this time, merchants in the said place.

These journeys were sometimes odd, such as the fourth which I undertook on my own during my time on the Coast, but this last journey was in the old service and business of the company. In order to install, at the same time and in line with the peculiar course of the times, the elected and recently accepted new Governor *"ad indesim"*, namely August Friderich Hachenberg, about whom not much more will be said in this place. He had been appointed in the absence of other more appropriate people in the service of the company. The last recreational journey to Fredensborg Fortress took place during the time of Christen Glob Dorph, a merchant at the place, which was and I hope, God willing, will be my most notable journey in this world until my eventual death and departure from this world.

[FREDERICUS'S DISTURBING MESSAGE ARRIVES FROM COPENHAGEN]

This extraordinary journey started on the 2nd of October in the year 1742 and exactly one month before, all appropriate provision had been made for this journey. For the undertaking of this said journey, the then Governor showed in this post, as in others earlier on, his usual politeness towards the domestic slaves of the company as regards carrying me and my luggage though tips and necessary provision for the necessities of the journey had to be held at my own expense. When I, on the second day, arrived at the Fortress of Fredensborg, I confess that I arrived to meet a very good friend, namely Monsieur Christen Glob Dorph, who displayed his usual friendship, helpfulness and good behaviour and also did not skimp on any of what was needed in order to receive and meet a visiting friend.

Indeed there were all imaginable proper and amusing pleasures. Still, although this journey of mine was for pleasure, as mentioned, I could not enjoy any pleasure in this place at all with the efforts to reasonably stave off my worries and in any way, my different and numerous many troubled and rather disturbing thoughts, which had originated from one mail which had been on board the ship "Grevinden af Haurvigen" (The Countess of Haurvigen). This ship had arrived at the Coast with very strict orders in a post about my person from the Honourable Gentlemen Directors which, Governor Jurgensen not only read to me but also showed to me to view so that I, with my own eyes, could see the Honourable Gentlemen Directors' strict and serious intentions concerning my person.

If my memory serves me right, the order from the Honourable Board ran along these lines: "The parish clerk, Frederik Svane, has requested his resignation as it is obvious that the Board has suffered many great expenses for his education and upbringing, to the effect that, as he is a native born in this country and familiar with its language, he could, most of all, be of benefit in helping to educate the youth in the local area and the country and this alone for the sake of his lusts of the flesh".

These were the distinct words of the order. Its last words made me corrupt in my head and mind as all the absolutely upright people on the Coast of Guinea - their lifestyle and nature - must freely and undoubtedly admit that there was an ungodly and carnally minded person, who demanded to rule and could have the same evil and impure lusts, and with most humble permission from Your

Excellencies and all the Honourable Gentlemen, tried to stop me from going back to Denmark.

To anybody who do not know the Coast of Guinea, I will say that in such warm climate of these warm countries, one must be there only for a short stay, As mentioned, there I saw the content of this strict and, in my opinion, absolutely irrevocable and irrefutable order, that, as any fair person can judge, I became so alarmed and unsettled that with my thoughts not being gathered on this matter, I did not know what on earth to do in order to have this so firmly tied knot undone. Having the unalterable, most unreasonable and thorough order from the Honourable Board changed and modified, could only make my poor head confused and disturbed.

While the ship, which had been carrying this strict order, was still at anchor below the Fortress, I had made a great effort and employed all imaginable diligence against the content of this incontrovertible order, to apply to the Administration for my so dearly wished for, and long overdue, expected resignation in case this should be a rescue for me. I was, I confess, and I could see this myself and my whole being after that time, that I was in such a miserable melancholy that I, and in particular, Mr Jurgensen the Governor, thought that I would lose my mind and senses. Yet, in spite of all this and regardless of how much the Governor and the entire Administration would have liked to have seen me being helped, my genuine friend Mr Christen Oluf Dorph, the former and now replaced and homeward bound clergyman, showed me his sincere faithfulness and made his greatest effort to bring about my dismissal so that I could leave.

Nevertheless, all of this was not sufficient to persuade Mr Jurgensen's kind soft-heartedness. Here, the order's requirement warranted that I, in the further demonstration of my then condition, made only a small stop and wait until a replacement came, which was for this good person and Clergyman, Mr Oluf Dorph, together with whom I had worked in the church service for four years as a Catechist and now as a caretaker Pastor, following the replacement of Mr Eric Trane whom, as mentioned previously, was succeeded in the benefice at Christiansborg, by the learned and honourable Mr Oluf Dorph as clergyman followed.

The *Theologian* Slave Trader

[FREDERICUS WRITES ABOUT PASTOR OLUF DORPH]

The second clergyman during my time at Christiansborg, in Guinea in Africa was learned etc. Mr Oluf Dorph who replaced former and homeward bound clergyman Eric Trane. The account of his arrival, start in the position, time in the position, life and living and eventual replacement, etc. is as follows. After the replacement of his predecessor and the journey back home the learned and honourable Mr Oluf Dorph continued in the benefice at the Fortress: a man who in life and living as well as in doctrine, conversation, composure and relations to his surroundings was a good man; one who was well-suited and well-placed particularly at Christiansborg and in that country.

As regards interpreting and explaining God's blessed words, he was a very well-read and experienced man who was full of thorough principles concerning the truths of the pure religion: beautifully blessed and most of all with moving admonitions for his trusted congregation "et subjectum", which was well suited for the coast of Guinea. He was very courteous towards his surroundings. He was helpful towards all the functionaries from the top, the Governor, to the most humble soldier not merely in terms of perpetual and sincere admonitions to lead a God-fearing and appropriate life by word and deed, but also in terms of the bodily necessities, by assisting everyone according to their means and salary, to achieve and negotiate the deserved income.

With regard to the foreign nations present on the coast, and the conversation with them, he was indeed courteous, respectful and polite as is right and suitable for a good clergyman. At his replacement and departure, I requested and obtained from this good friend, though be it in a verbal form, as at this point I was confused in my head and did not have the wherewithal to make an appropriate written request, for his testimony and reference for my affairs during the time I had been in the service of the church together with him. The attestation he gave me can be found in the written attestation given me by his predecessor Mr Trane whom I most respectfully refer to.

I have now lingered for some time on this good clergyman's life and affairs on the coast during his entire time. On occasion of Your Excellency's most graciously issued order to me, I must in the most clear and truthful manner, without any doubt and regret, in the briefest manner, to continue my own living and conduct's trustworthy description hereafter as before with the most dutiful humbleness in the most scrupulously and most accurate way to comply with the following, my previously mentioned, most peculiar journey to Fredensborg Fortress, which took its start in 1742 and had a dual purpose, partly for myself and partly for the Administration. As regards the general purpose of the journey for the Administration, the following was the case. One month previously, a peculiar misunderstanding had arisen between the then Administration consisting of Governor Mr Peder Nicolaj Jurgensen, merchant Christen Glob Dorph and the bookkeeper Hans Hansen Blass.

[FREDERICUS ATTEMPTS TO MAKE PEACE AMONGST THE OFFICIALS AT CHRISTIANSBORG]

There was a terribly tiresome and soon implacable antagonism, which, in case it should persist, could seemingly lead to the most difficult and precarious circumstances for the meanest and most harmful consequences in its wake, not merely for themselves but even, in the worst case, for the entire respectable company and their graciously entrusted undertakings and affairs and rule, in the case that the said people did not receive advice in time and were not checked and calmed down.

Therefore, I was considering this misfortune not only from the perspective of a Parish Clerk in the service of the Company, but in accordance to my sworn duty and most humble obligation towards the most respectable company. They were duties, which I always considered and carefully fulfilled in these very precarious circumstances at the Fortress Christiansborg and thus I acted as a mediator between the honourable gentlemen and with the most possible diligence, I worked at making these disputing minds reconciled with each other, not merely for the common good of themselves but mostly for the benefit of the Company there. In doing so, I did in no way attempt to seek any personal gain or particular advantage for myself which might be honest and innocent.

With God's help, I had now at Christiansborg Fortress managed to prepare the ground for hope for the repair of the desirable and close friendship between the then disagreeing people, namely the Governor Jurgensen and Hans Hansen Blass, the bookkeeper who is still amongst us. As far as I have been informed, he resides in this town (Copenhagen). However, this result was not achieved to the extent that I had in mind and for which I was applying my diligence and care as Christen Glob Dorph, the merchant at the Fortress Fredensborg and the second vote in the Secret Privy-Council, was not present but was to be found at his entrusted Fortress Fredensborg. For this and other reasons I, who made it my task to create peace and agreement between the disputing parties, was obliged to embark on a journey to Fredensborg Fortress at Ningo.

Having arrived safely at Fredensborg Fortress at the end of September, I was received and approached with sincerity and courtesy by my very good friend, Christen Glob Dorph. At the first available opportunity, I presented the reason for my journey, which was very incumbent to me, to him and the other highly determined gentlemen. He listened to my well-meaning proposition and my intention of good and desirable closeness and relations between the Board and it's Administration on the Coast of Guinea. I promised my good intentions and full devotion to the company's benefit and prosperity and assured him that in his case he should do everything for the sake of building real peace and friendship and conversation between him and the two other previously mentioned Honourable Gentlemen in the Administration, namely Mr Jurgensen and Monsieur Blass, that he could rest assured on them as they could on him.

Thus, there existed no hindrance, which could or should have given cause for even the smallest misunderstanding and disagreement between them. However, he did say, that it was very difficult for him to believe in Governor Jurgensen as he had previously made it clear that he, namely Dorph, along with Hans Blass, had conspired between them to have him dethroned and dismissed from the Administration.

Gracious Master! The misunderstanding appeared so very dangerous that Jurgensen so quickly should have changed into believing in, and relating to, Christen Dorph as a friend in confidence, at a second vote in the Privy-Council. Yet if Dorph, according to my plans, was assured of a good change in Jurgensen's unstable temperament, then nothing remained in the way of building a good friendship and its continuation provided that two other people in the Administration as well as several other civilian functionaries at the Fortress Christiansborg, would be with us all here at Ningo so we could, better here than at Christiansborg, consider all these matters for the best purpose and in order to create a pleasant friendship and maintenance of it. He could well, Dorph added, write to Christiansborg Fortress in order to invite them to come to him at Fredensborg. Yet, he knew very well that this would not be of any use as they only had little trust in him, that he would have changed into a confident and sincere friend of them.

In my mind, I believed that they, on the other side, had absolutely no cause to harbour any doubts, as I was assured. I thought to myself that this was a matter about which everything would be decided at Christiansborg Fortress. Upon this, Dorph sat down to write a letter to both of the disputing parties. Its content was an invitation, if they would be so kind as to undertake a journey to Ningo in order for him to present urgent matters. Yet they, contrary to my hopes and in accordance with Mr Christen Glob Dorph's previously held opinions, did not come, but did merely rejected with a polite refusal his kind and well-meaning invitation. This ended his previously conceived positive thoughts about the change of their minds into that of friendship and trust. This was, amongst all of them, ruled a dangerous distrust and suspicious ideas which, when I heard of, I must confess, put my mind and thoughts in a state of great confusion as if of a strong sign of the inconstancy of a mortal human being in this world where, every day, you can see and hear nothing but mere inconstancy in all creations.

This did convince me, more so than for some time, not to put any substantial faith in anything in nature, other than in the unalterable God, as the Prophet says in the world beyond: "By Him exists no change or shadow of change" but what was there for me to do? To withdraw one's hand from the creation of this reconciliation and accord seemed to me shameful. Also inside myself there existed such inconstancy, that I should not make use of by any further imaginable means towards a good reconciliation and repair of friendship in these differing personalities.

The first solution and the one closest at hand was also the best now. According to my spirit and nature as a man of action, I had to act according to my nature and strike while the iron was still hot. Therefore, having quickly made my decision, I once again turned my thoughts to those two, Jurgensen and Dorph, so quickly changing men, Governor Jurgensen in particular. I did so in order to see, if it would be possible to make them properly reconciled and to make them go to Ningo, which also happened.

Yet, before our very stately and considerable long journey and the splendid arrival at Fredensborg Fortress and the reception by Mr Christen Glob Dorph, the merchant, it occurs to me that I should add a couple of words here to mention my own particular reason which urged me to initiate and complete this journey. The reason was that for some time, I had been so very troubled that I hardly believed I should be able to stay sane. This was very much owing to the order which had been issued to my person from the Honourable Board in Copenhagen stating that I, if nothing more reasonably could be determined, should be forced, like a slave, to stay in the country and spend my entire and possibly very short life so miserably and deplorably away from my dear wife and son who, according to a close examination of the order, could not be expected to join me due to the ideas and objectives of this order.

I was forever and always thinking about this and related issues and I wondered in particular about the authority and power of the Board to force me against my will. Yet, in order to adjust myself to this very reasonable proposal and aim for me, I began thinking, what was unreasonable and to God, incomprehensible to continue to be unwilling to go along with this, but found in fact, that it was agreeable to accommodate my mind according to their gracious intentions and will. Therefore, I had to get used to a complacent willingness and turn my need into a virtue. Upon this rapid resolution, I became so overly happy and pleased in my miserable mind, that I hardly knew how to accustom myself to these so hastily occurred and delightful thoughts about this reconciliation

[FREDERICUS PLANS TO BUILD A MANSION FOR HIS WIFE AND SON]

In this imaginary affection, I began to fabricate several new and serious whims and, at the time, unnecessary provisions for the planning and building of a necessary house for my convenience, for myself and my due wife and son, in the event that I should find mercy before the Honourable Directors so that I could, at least, bring them back to join me again; something, which the issued order did not bring much hope for.

This new resolve about my humble house and the ensuing future facilities made me so cheerful that I decided not to hide my heart's secret delight over this but was contemplating the best way and the most rightful manner in which to let this be known so that other people too could share the delight and pleasure of this joy which was swelling up within me, considering the sincere admonition of the Apostles "To share one's joy with each other".

[FREDERICUS ORGANIZES A LAVISH PARTY WITH GOLD ORNAMENTS AS GIFTS]

To create even more joy and pleasure for my imagined friends, I made all the necessary efforts in order to do everything one could think of to delight the honest and respectable company at a party. There upon, I immediately opened, by God's blessing, my previously acquired treasure, a small gold box and weighed out from it 32 Rigsdaler (Rdl.), in order for the goldsmith to manufacture for me 16 Rdl. gold for a head on a narrow cane walking stick which I had purchased for myself recently and 16 Rdl. for pure gold rings to give away over and during the festivities and the banquet. I should also have liked to have had music yet the soldier and tailor at the Fortress who acted as a musician playing a fiddle was playing such sad and miserable music that it grated badly on my ears and therefore I thought that it could not please anybody else either, although he then played beautifully into the ears of Governor Jurgensen.

As I had now made complete preparations to my liking, I travelled with this most stately and splendid group and party consisting of Mr Peter Nicolaj Jurgensen, the Governor; Monsieur Hans Hansen Blass, the Bookkeeper; Simon Hendrick Klein, Ludvig Ferdinand Romer and August Friderich Hachenberg, the first assistant, whereof the last three Monsieurs were present although they were not involved in the previously mentioned dispute in the Administration. Yet I had invited them and brought them along. This was partly for my own pleasure and at my own expense as I considered them to be my genuine friends, especially Monsieur Romer with whom I had hitherto enjoyed a close friendship and partly because the presence of these gentlemen would make my planned festivities and banquet all the more splendid.

As mentioned, on the second of October, I managed with much effort to get the very honourable and respectable group to travel with me to Fredensborg Fortress. In the meantime, the then Reverend Mr Peder Meyer was kind enough to perform my duties in my absence at Christiansborg Fortress so that nothing should be neglected for that reason.

This very stately group was escorted by a large number of black slaves at my expense for the purpose of carrying the journey's necessary equipage and ourselves, in addition to the Company's slaves, whom the Governor had arranged for this purpose; we travelled up from Christiansborg Fortress when the evening approached. Then the shining stars began to emerge and let their clear light brighten up the dark and unpleasant night which sweet and refreshing dew quenched and delighted us during the entire night, whilst we were on the journey, until the first blush of dawn and the clear light of the firmament beamed towards us as a groom from his chamber. So did this splendid group approach the Fortress with the lovely sun's most wonderful rays of light shining towards the Fortress Fredensborg at Ningo.

After we had arrived at Fredensborg Fortress, the first day passed with conversation and entertainment. Even so, much discussion and deliberation regarding the issues of misunderstanding and disagreement inside the Administration were taking place. Sometimes they did so under four eyes and sometimes again in public for everybody there to hear. Everything was presented thoroughly and everyone's perspectives were brought to the fore with the aim of building and maintaining a genuine and lasting friendship, a good reconciliation, agreement, real affection and good relations amongst them in the best possible manner, and by use of the most moving and persuasive words whereby I achieved my wished for goal, very well.

This very important friendship had finally been established and no imaginable effort and diligence could spare me in order to achieve a stable continuation. On the second day after a solution had been reached at Fredensborg Fortress, my particularly good friend, the local merchant Mr Dorph, hosted a decent banquet and a meal arranged by him and funded by myself. In lacking music during the banquet, I supplied the vocal music myself and presented as best as I could a particular aria about God's great mercifulness and strange gracious guidance and company, from the time of my tender childhood and reflecting on my melancholic thoughts that I had lost my father all too early. Then, as a small child of tender age, I had to become accustomed to life as a fatherless child and almost motherless too, in a poor life with many and varied changes caused by changing luck. I was then bearing in mind God's great protection and fatherly care through his special providence in the world hence forth, and not merely regarding necessary food and clothing every day, but also regarding the true nourishment of the soul with a blessed and necessary education for the purpose of achieving a good life after this through the humble work by his most faithful servant, the chosen tool, Elias Svane, my honourable father before God, who had created me as "Paul" carried out his mission with much pain of a Clergyman's Godlike and true diligence, with fatherly care and education.

I endured all these hardships in the Christian and purely blessed doctrine's most pure and precious truths until I became favoured and privileged and his most divine majesty granted me the most privileged charge on the coast of Guinea. I worked as a Parish Clerk and Catechist in the service of the company at Christiansborg Fortress. This had taken shape during many and varied changes and occurrences which, I confess, were rather exhausting and, to me, difficult fatalities and troubles. For this improvised aria, if I may use this word for my humble thoughts, I took the opportunity of using "Samuel's" confession in the next world when the Lord blessed his Israel with the glorious victory over his enemies, then the river carried its superfluous tides into the sea like a source of gratitude for its wholesomeness. The Prophet cried out significantly, "Eben Eser, Eben Eser, hitherto the Lord has helped, praises alone to God".

Afterwards, the gold rings which had been prepared for this occasion, were presented on a plate at the table and distributed to the highly esteemed dining guests who were seated there, starting with the Governor; Mr Dorph the merchant and Hans Hansen Blass and their accompanying negro women and then Romer, Klein, Hackenberg and Laurids Bay, who were deputy-assistants, and the one at Ningo, Simon Klein, was the one of all the assistants who had, some time previously, taken in a negro woman who also received a ring. Each member of the Administration and the Council received two rings, and the others received one each.

Around the table, my personal future building plans were discussed and, without having been prompted, they all urged on me, and without any demands in return, their help and suggested their assistance, and agreed that, it was best that I made a start right away as soon as I arrived back at Christiansborg Fortress and the occasion now arose for me where it would be convenient and advantageous to build. I found all the highest ranking people in the service of the Company present at the Fortress Fredenborg and the Administration, in favour of supporting the completion of such a building which, they said, perhaps would be difficult for me to begin and carry out with a satisfactory result on my own.

Governor Jurgensen, being the highest ranking and most important person amongst all the guests in this very respectable party, offered his special and particular goodwill towards my good enterprise by pledging 50 Rdl. for this purpose as a genuine gift from a friend. In addition, he promised to assist me with some necessary building materials from the "Flinte Kister" - (flint boxes with building materials from Denmark), owned by the Fortress, for floors, ceiling, doors, windows and other necessities for this purpose. Immediately, the bookkeeper, Monsieur Hans Hansen Blass, followed suit and he too offered a present of 50 Rdl. for the assistance and help for this project. Mr Christen Glob Dorph also presented me with a gift of a male slave immediately on the same day and a carriage.

Indeed, they all showed how pleased they were with me that they were, in fact, competing with each other about who should keep on doing good for me and nobody seemed to be able to do enough and so wanted to do even more for me. All these blessed and desirable offers were promised me, and I accepted with the most humble and abject gratefulness, which made me believe that this building which I had in mind was not just a dream, but a strong reality since I had only recently made my decision about it.

Before starting the work, it would have to be well thought out and planned with the necessary preparations and materials as it was bad to start at something, which one could not complete over time. While such conversation was passing over the table, a very beautiful and delicate verse was produced by Monsieur Simon Klein, and was composed by the group according to my nature and state of mind, so that these highly respectable gentlemen could take pleasure and delight in this, instead of confectionery.

After the dinner, I handed out presents, "panchise", to everybody's slave servant-boys, to everyone right from the highest ranking Governor's servant-boy to those belonging to the most low ranking personnel. Also to the local Constable who was my brother I gave a gold ring, and some garments to his wife, for the effort he had made to help me. To other negro women and other slave boy-servants, I gave two "panchise" presents each.

When a couple of days of pleasant visiting at the Fortress Fredensborg had come to an agreeable end, the Governor again turned his thoughts back to Christiansborg Fortress and on the morning of the third day he returned with his considerably big accompanying party from Ningo. The Governor's departure from this most honourable party, and its accompanying very respectable company, was also followed, a little later, by the merchant, Mr Christen Glob Dorph, and his assistant, Laurids Bay and myself.

[FREDERICUS GOES ON BOARD A FRENCH SLAVE SHIP TO SELL SLAVES]

I had intended to stay a few more days at Fredensborg Fortress for a little recreation though this was only for a short time, since just a few days later a message came through to Ningo from Christiansborg Fortress which declared that, at Accra, on the shores off Christiansborg Fortress, a vessel was at anchor with a Frenchman who negotiated and traded in slaves. Immediately thereafter, Mr Christen Glob Dorph requested from me if I would, on this occasion, undertake business on his behalf at Accra. The business being that I should travel to Accra as soon as possible and take with me, on his behalf, two slaves to be traded on board the French vessel there. I could not refuse this business, as he, Mr Dorph, was a friend. I took upon myself to carry out this request and towards the evening of the same day, I left Ningo and on the second day thereafter, I arrived at Christiansborg Fortress at mid-morning around 10 o'clock. The following day, I was getting prepared, having received the Governor's permission, to go on board the French vessel.

However, the Administration at Fredensborg Fortress had now persuaded me to build my planned house and preferably doing so sooner rather than later. When the good occasion now arose that the Administration would help me with money as well as materials I thought that such a good occasion should not be missed here. Upon this, I summoned my boldness and requested from the Governor, Jurgensen, if he could show me his kindness by lending me a male slave until the payment had to be made "in goods" or with another good slave as I should now like to make a start on my building. For this he showed me his favour.

I had I said, furthermore, two small boys whom I would also market and sell on in case I could get any decent and adequate payment for them. Likewise here, I said, I have two male slaves on behalf of Mr Dorph, the merchant at Fredensborg, whom I should sell on his behalf which he, the Governor, also permitted. Afterwards, I went on board and negotiated and sold the mentioned five slaves, namely, three for myself, one man and two boys, and two for the merchant, Mr Dorph. Later, I arrived safely and happily back on land with my acquired goods in return for the above mentioned five slaves and I even became richer after our outstanding account, regarding the advance and outlay which he had made for my entertainment at Ningo.

I then immediately began to make preparations as to what was necessary for this building: iron tools to break up stones with; large stones for the foundations and smaller stones for the wall and even much smaller ones to fill the gaps in between the larger stones and I also made preparations to have clay mixed. From the Governor's servant boy, namely Captain Noy, I purchased the summerhouse, which had belonged to the former Governor Boris, but had been given to him, Captain Noy, by Mr Jurgensen. I paid for this summerhouse with a cask of French distilled spirits which, when it was sold, would fetch 24 Rdl. and much more in "Boss", a local trading currency. I had the house pulled down so that its stones could be used for my building. I also let stones, wherever they could be found, be brought to my chosen, and assigned by the Administration, site. This was close to the garden of the former Governor Boris, in a valley below the Fortress Christiansborg, situated right at the side of the houses for the Company's slaves, which in that part of the country, were called "Casas".

[FREDERICUS STARTS HIS BUILDING PROJECT IN EARNEST]

Indeed, great expensive stones were carried from Labadi by Negroes dependent on the Fortress, from a quarter, if not half a mile, of the way to the Fortress Christiansborg. (a Danish mile = 4.68 British statute miles). They located, broke loose and obtained all the stones they could find and managed to bring from everywhere, for the mentioned building site so that together, I had more than thirty great heaps of stones which had been brought over and carefully arranged in order to be conveniently at hand for the master builders to take as they needed them.

A considerable quantity of clay was in good supply, that is, as much as I imagined would be needed knowing that I, when the time came, might otherwise lack water for this because in that period, namely October, November, December and January, a strong heat and a penetrating drought could occur. In short, I had prepared myself for all the things that I could imagine in advance not merely to begin the work with, but also in order to continue and complete this projected building. I had ordered trees in advance for timber, when required, and had decided as to where from it should come. I had thought of all the things that would be necessary in order to begin and complete such a building.

This was a very considerable preparation which immediately caused much attention and many kinds of pointless worries on several occasions for many unfounded and untruthful conversations, and unwarranted, unreasonable, thoughtless, yes, indeed, rather awfully dangerous ideas and assumptions, which, had made the then Administration the laughing stock on the entire coast of Guinea, amongst both white and black alike in Africa. This shall most humbly be referred, in more detail, for more sensibly and just people, particularly to Your Excellency and the Gentlemen Directors.

For the sake of clarity, I reminded myself of the continuation of my particular current affairs. All the said considerable preparations and materials for my mentioned projected building were not merely approved by the Administration at Fredensborg Fortress at Ningo, but the members even strongly animated such a completion with the most desirable promises of help, instigated by their own favour and positive attention towards me, which, in the previous account of my entertaining and the banquet at Fredensborg Fortress was, as one could see, obviously not arranged by me without great expense.

At first, I had with the good grace of God, in order to save any possible unnecessary expense, procured my own male slave for the initial preparations of this work and, since his biological brother turned out to be amongst the company's slaves at the Christansborg Fortress, my slave requested if I would possibly see to having his brother released from the Fortress to himself, as he committed himself to even more faithful and willing service to me when his brother was released to him. As I was their master at the house, they would have great opportunity to prove all possible and united faithful service which, given his continuing and well-intended request, I could not at all refuse. As soon as possible, I therefore set about to arrange the release and completed it, though this was done with good credit by Mr Jurgensen.

These two brother-slaves and my own slaves continued to work every day, dragging large stones from wherever they could manage to find some: from the fields, from the beach, from the gardens, from the square and from wherever else they could find stones which were suitable for building work. In addition, I had my own woman slave whom I was keeping so that food could be prepared for these two brothers so that the most necessary meals could be prepared and be ready for them right away on their return from work and in order that they would not have to spend time on such things which would have caused a delay in my planned work on the building. With wholly adequate wages, I had hired Negroes from the village of Osu, or the Negro settlement, to hack loose, dig and mix a considerable amount of clay in order to have good provisions, not merely to lay the planned foundations, but also for the future use in the building's continuation and its near completion. Each day, I had a considerable amount of the village people who carried broken up stones, not only to be taken to the building site from the Labadi Negro settlement, as explained earlier, but also for the construction work itself which was already established, praise be to God, and continued well for me.

Yet, it was a shame that nobody, especially my mighty enemies who were in fact to be found in the Administration, took part in this my great pleasure, despite their own earlier instigation or their own undeniable enthusiasm for this project during the meeting at Fredensborg Fortress. Indeed, this applied even more so to Governor Jurgensen who was still amongst us and residing in this very Christiansborg Fortress and, not only him but also Monsieur Blass, the Bookkeeper, had at Ningo, given me such delightful encouragement and a promise of a gift of 50 Rdl towards my building. They had even given me the Company's own and then available master builder at Christiansborg Fortress permission to work on this construction though it be for money and a good payment on accord of 6 Rdl per month, besides food and similar provisions and for supervising the black people in order that everything should be done properly, and that straight and even walls should be erected without any depressions or even the smallest of flaws and errors, as I should like to make this building as perfect as possible.

The foundations had already been laid and almost an entire foot of the wall upwards had been built in just a few days, a square of two by three feet in the groundwork and later it became more reduced as it went upwards. According to my projected plans, the construction should have three storeys and a garden should be added around the house for pleasure and recreation. My biggest error at this time and place, I confess, was that I was exceedingly cheerful and pleased, so that I had all the more pleasure for myself. The working master builders let a small Negro hut just opposite the building site, be repaired so that we, when the mighty midday sun fell upon us with its penetrating heat and warmth, could retreat to this hut for safe shelter. This was also a convenient place in that it served as our dining room and sitting room.

In this thatched house I had also followed an impulse from my overly happy mood which, I do admit, was a quite fantastic and an amazing idea. I had had a pole erected similar to a flagpole. And to this pole, I had let my boys attach a white canvass sheet, which was painted and marked with the Danish flag in the upper right comer. All these above mentioned preparations and materials, Your Gracious Excellency and Honourable Directors, for such a house at such a place and in such a country would not have been made to this degree and standard without the waste and expense of a very considerable sum of money. The extent of these expenses for the preparations of the house and the making of its foundations, besides offering food in accordance with the country's customs to the Negroes in the Negro settlement, can more easily be described here in a hasty and brief manner with a few words, than by calculating and doing the sums.

[FREDERICUS IS ACCUSED OF BEING A TRAITOR]

As the building of my planned house, its necessary preparations and the laying of the foundations were now in such energetic progress and continued with such a desirable pace at my own expense and modest circumstances, though be it, with God's blessing and wonderful providence, with undeniable continuation and progress, such blessings created many enemies for me. Those enemies, envious persecutors, quite corrupted and confused in their senseless, brainless and corrupted dumb heads, since those envious devils themselves owned nothing, so they had also nothing to concern themselves with besides that some one else has been blessed by God with means in order to meet his needs.

This was exactly what happened to me this time with the blessing granted to me by God. I encountered envy and hostility even from those in whom I certainly had expected the greatest friendship and whom I had used the most possible diligence trying to serve them night and day. Concerning that which passed, I acknowledged that I sometimes, to my own great harm and disadvantage and, chiefly with Mr Jurgensen, the Governor and Colony Manager, whose man I always had to be, be it at night or at day time, I confess I was always ready and willing to assist him with advice although the circumstances had not always been, God alone be praised, adequate for me in my present position, to be good enough for a Governor to ask for advice from a Parish Clerk at Christiansborg Fortress. Although I, on several occasions, acknowledged from unfailing knowledge and experience, that my good advice was sometimes worth money. However, my services for Mr Jurgensen were not merely giving advice which, I have to say, was nevertheless so good that Mr Jurgensen, in case he was a sensible and wise Governor, could have taken the good guidance from it but whether he had made use of such services only he knows.

This big preparation caused much attention at Christiansborg Fortress because at the same time my salary book showed that the Company was due a considerable amount whereof a part was deducted from my payment, for garments and other necessities which had been purchased last September at an auction which had

The *Theologian* Slave Trader

taken place at the Fortress following a reserve from the Secretary, namely Hans Steen, who was associated with Mr Christen Glob Dorph at Ningo but died at Christiansborg Fortress. Some of these goods were purchased in anticipation of my building work. I had 12 casks of French distilled spirits and some of this was consumed during the work on the building. Some of them were traded in 'Boss', a local currency for the daily workers in order to continue this project, and a good deal of goods were traded for gold and money for the same purpose. The members of the Administration, and perhaps also some of the functionaries in the service of the Fortress and the Company, I should not say all of them, looking at and contemplating this big and fairly considerable building work with its necessary preparations and one never knew what thoughts they had on the subject, forgot all their unprompted, previously extended, offers of help for my building.

Sometimes they had so many unreasonably bad ideas such as: I had a pixie or a small devil in my room at the Fortress who would bring me money or gold for my project. I found most of them were persisting and they also said, that one of my slaves, while digging up stones, found a pot of gold and had brought it to me along with other things; such were the assumptions. They were thinking first of all, that I, a poor and unwise building owner, had started this construction work without thought or consideration, without any prior premeditation as to whether I would also be able to complete this work. However, when they saw that everything had a desirable progress and, that for each day that passed, work went yet faster, then they put their heads together and began to consider how they might disrupt this work. In order to carry out their vile plot, they planned an untruthful and irresponsible fabrication: that my previously mentioned journey to Ningo and the entertainment in this place did not happen for the reason which was given, but that I and Mr Christen Glob Dorph, who were so close good friends, had other motives.

Their aim was, in particular, that the Governor Jurgensen should be put to a strange disadvantage and harm and that Mr Dorph's previously promised assistance meant also that, building the house, was assisted by him, which they, the functionaries, in their whims and ideas, made a big issue out of.

Their best goal, they thought, namely the Governor along with Monsieur Blass the bookkeeper, and probably more people in the service at the Fortress, who envied my success, was to build up misunderstanding and disagreement between myself and Mr Dorph. It was their aim to conjure up something, which would occupy me with other affairs than my building work. An aim this vile group set up to achieve right away. Quickly, they wrote to Fredensborg in order to let Mr Dorph know that they had learned with certainty that he and the Parish Clerk Friederich had conspired together and had planned dangerous schemes towards the Administration which they wanted to overturn together and to take over the authority to great and wide reaching harm. Other even more crude, unfounded and unreasonable excesses of accusations became known on Mr Dorph's arrival from Ningo to Christiansborg Fortress.

When Mr Dorph had learned about the aforementioned statement, he had immediately, and without any hesitation, set out on a journey to Christiansborg Fortress in order to deny all responsibility for these dangerous, false, and fabricated claims. What happened then? The following took place: the official Court at Christiansborg Fortress was set and I was taken from my work unexpectedly, without having received any summons, and brought before the Court to answer questions in this case, to hear witnesses and to receive a sentence. I had no previous knowledge about any of these accusations, as I, an innocent man, arrived straight from my work at the Fortress, which was then closed off. Upon this I found myself in the Governor's hall where I unexpectedly saw them sitting in justice and I was charged with the previous, untruthful allegations, false and invented accusations.

Upon this, I defended myself, which was reasonable, with the most transparent and sensible proofs and explanations such as Governor Jurgensen's great kindness and occasional particular confidence and kind affection for which I was envied; the attention and special honour which is bestowed on me for my well meaning sincerity towards him which was displayed on some difficult occasions in the Administration; special compliance, obedient, humility, loyalty, modesty and defence of the honour of the Governorship with ingenious and continuing good advice to venerate his authority and good reputation and protect him against all slander and contempt which was not right for a Governor, to defend and exercise peculiarity for him, with respects to the dangerous fear of being dethroned from the Administration. My untiring diligence and loyal efforts, indeed at a great expense, were in order to establish and continue a friendship and good confidence in the Administration which can be seen in the previous account about our arrival to Fredensborg Fortress and other statements of the same nature.

I presented these to the Court based on which the court could probably easily decide contrary to these unfounded accusations against my innocent person. In spite of this I was nevertheless, without any legal basis, sentenced quite objectionably and unlawfully to abandon not only my planned building, but also not to receive the payment of two month's salary as a penalty for my offence. I was then considering the Administration's unlawful treatment of me and learned about the real and truthful reason for this fabrication against me. So, I confess that I declared out right that I would not comply with this unlawful and unfounded sentence that was based on a falsely fabricated and untruthful case. Yet, if I, contrary to my good intentions, should be wronged although I was innocent, they might as well extend the fine as much and as far as they pleased. Then they should rather take some extra months' salary from me as this was, I said, altogether better than taking two or twenty-four Rdl. from me. Indeed, they were entirely at liberty to decide if they would, through power, force me to give them everything that might be due to me since it was obvious to me that they were simply seeking to bring about my ruin and depravity.

Overcome by a rather shameful conscience, they then immediately began to destroy their recently passed sentence. They tore it up before the public in the Court, as it was written on loose paper and they revoked it so that I should be free from this sentence. However, I should give up my building as I had a good quarter, a 'casa' in the Fortress and was in the service of the Company and did not at all, therefore, require this kind of house especially in my presently single state. However, this kind of injustice and unlawful procedure and treatment of an innocent person by the Administration at Christiansborg Fortress, was carried out in order to disrupt my planned work in spite of all things,

I did nevertheless and, with God's protection, continue this much wanted building work of mine in order to complete it. Yet I went through pains and difficulties in my efforts to overcome the troubles and obstacles that were occurring from time to time during this period that were instigated by my powerful enemies, in order to achieve the goal I desired. This was hopefully going to be a peaceful home in this so very un-peaceful world, thanks to the plans of the building, suitable for living in such a house. In the following, the Gracious Gentlemen Directors will be given further evidence of this.

It did not suffice for my powerful enemies and merciless opponents to put such hindrances in my way and my building work; they were not tired, instead they persevered. They continued to prepare their evil intentions and false pretexts every day and they did not stop disrupting this construction but attempted even to bring my person to fall and to be disgraced. Since this first vile, fabricated attack had failed, then this doubly troublesome and dangerous invention was made up, namely that I was threatening the life and wellbeing of Governor Mr Jurgensen. In addition, that my intention with this prepared, initiated and arranged building work should not have been the innocent aim which I had explained, to build an ordinary home, but much more than that, in fact, into a Fortress and stronghold and, in this way, to take revenge and bring malice and ruin to the company's Fortress and stronghold, Christiansborg. Oh, all the bad injustice in this world! Oh, this inhuman cruelty! Oh, this insatiable greed! The purpose of their murderous fabrication could easily have concluded to have been to sacrifice my humble life and blood. Why?

When I realised this to the full extent and from the widespread rumour which had been convinced about this evil plot's most dangerous consequences and I, 'God forgive me', so despaired in my mind, I resolved to take my own life in order that I could finally reach the end of this troublesome life.

In such despairing thoughts and a strongly growing melancholy, I went for a walk on the battery and came passed the soldiers' quarters and, at that very moment, I noticed Johannes Klein, the brother of Monsieur Simon Hendrich Klein, enjoying a glass of French distilled spirits. He called me over and asked if I would not like to join him? I answered, "Yes, I do". He then poured a glass for me, which I drank. Then he asked me if I would like one more drink. I said yes. I continued in this manner until I had consumed one and a half bottles of distilled spirits. Although this was a very strong drink indeed, yet, in my severe melancholy and desperation, this was so weak that to me it did not taste any stronger than cold water. Out of sheer desperation, I wanted this strong drink to aid my voluntary death.

[FREDERICUS'S FIRST ARREST NOVEMBER 1742]

From this strong drink, I became quite confused and I walked straight up to Mr Jurgensen in his hall and said, I have heard that the Governor has been told that I, with my building, am aimed at having the Fortress Christiansborg demolished and him Mr Jurgensen not merely dethroned, but even threatened on his life and well-being and, from this, I said, it was obvious to see and conclude what the members of the Administration finally were intending to do to me, namely, to make an attempt on my life and blood with this most vile and corrupted plot. If this was the case, I requested most humbly, if not it would please the Governor to sue me in an impartial Court here at the lawful Company's Fortress and stronghold, Christiansborg, where the case could be handled in a legal and regular manner. Truthful witnesses could then be produced against me according to the law and, in the event that I was found to be guilty of such intentions and evil actions, then they could subject me to such a punishment as is stated in the law.

But what happened then? Though I presented all of this to Mr Jurgensen, I have to admit, this was probably done in a manner less appropriate than I ought to have done, as at this moment in time, I was in an improper constitution and condition as the aforementioned drinking of strong spirits, also this condition I was in might have made me say a few words which, I would never be uttering neither before nor after in my entire life. This, quite understandably, had robbed me of my faculties' full use. The Governor then shouted down his hall for the guard ordering that I should be taken to my room with shackles on hands and feet and be taken out into custody in my own room like a prisoner. This also did happen.

Strangely, this was done with such zeal and bitterness that, with the split pin on the hand shackle, they perforated the wrist on my right hand, which left a visible and irremovable scar for the rest of my life. The next day when I had regained my senses, I found myself in custody with shackles on both hands and feet and the perforated wrist had covered me in blood. I confess and do not deny that I, in order to get my clothes back, broke the shackles and put on clean clothes. When these clothes were later on found and presented to the Governor this episode had such an effect on him that I was moved and taken from my own room into the ordinary, most common and low cell called the "Black Hole", where I had to spend the night.

However, at some point in the night, I was overcome by a strong sense of impatience that provided me with such strength that I, yet again, broke the shackles. On the second day after this, I was brought into the hall before the Governor who, on this occasion, proved himself much more gentle towards me than on the previous day and he merely confronted me with my daring behaviour in his quarters with all its noise and alarm in the hall which was not proper. He then demanded that I behaved as I used to do and he acknowledged that he did not believe what had been reported to him about me: that it was for me, impossible to make an attempt on his life. I admitted to my condition on the previous day. I acknowledged my guilt and then asked for forgiveness.

Because of all these above mentioned strange procedures against me, I was now almost as unhappy at Christiansborg Fortress as I could possibly become. I requested my final dismissal from and by the service of the Company as I could no longer expect and hope for any safety for my life. This plea and request, which I had often repeated, was at first refused by Mr Jurgensen but later on he did consider this and finally promised me this. However, I would have to await for this for another few days which was the final vile action which Christiansborg Fortress, even at my dismissal from the service, had reserved the right to harm and damage me. I then took up my work as I had done before and continued my efforts on the building.

Yet, when I had really gained pace and was hence making progress, the last obstacle was concocted against me because of the same work. This had the following course of action which will be clear from the following brief account of my last pitiful, innocent and regrettable arrest and will be described most humbly thus:

> *a most truthful account of my involuntary sentence into custody, for half a year and two weeks at the Fortress Christiansborg at the end of November in the year1742, until the middle of June in the year 1743, which was unlawful for God and man according to God's law of nations, and also against the laws of the high Gentlemen Directors.*

Your Excellency! All the Honourable Gentlemen Directors from the High Royal Privileged Danish, West Indian-Guinea Coast Company! Gracious Lords! In spite of these powerful and peculiar hindrances in order to deflect me from this my desirable work, I nevertheless continued my work on my building and did not let my hands rest or my courage fade. I did so because I always believed in my God who had always helped me, his unworthy servant, and that He would continue to be by my side, otherwise, I would be lost. Still, one should bear in mind, that nobody can hinder what God wants to promote and vice versa; nobody can promote what God wants to hinder and set back. Therefore, as mentioned, I became as "Nehemiah" from all of these "Samaritans" and "Caana's" children's mighty hindrances, not at all disrupted and held back but did instead, seem to be favoured by an apparently Divine blessing and situation. As regards the disheartened Fortress, to my mind, and as someone who did not have much business with the honourable Administration at Christiansborg Fortress anymore, as they only had little and poor faith in me and therefore could not tolerate me in their presence and also, for the sake of my own safety, I did no longer demand to be amongst them there.

The reason? From their false and unfounded madness and imagined suspicions about my unproven murderous intentions towards themselves, I could surely conclude and predict for myself, how evil their plans were and how murderous they were towards me in their hearts even though I had hopes of so much kindness from them as they did from me. I confess freely before the face of God with my conscience as witness, 1 had deserved so much kindness from which is demonstrated clearly in the previous part of this present and, for the all-seeing God, as the general account clearly shows, in particular the laborious diligence, great effort and expense, in order to create a reconciliation and appeasement between the Administration and Fredensborg Fortress at Ningo.

While I now, as mentioned, persevered with my building work under the Divine Majesty's strangely gracious providence, happiness and blessing, the concerned Administration was not sitting idle either, but was meditating over what would be useful to them in order to hinder me from working and thus cause great harm and ruin. A reason would necessarily have to be found, as one must have a ground for a building although this would sometimes be a sandy ground which is poor for building on, due to the hastily occurring stormy winds. Sometimes, a morass would be uncertain to build on as the weak roof of the rising building could over time suppress the building into its poor ground, much to its own disgrace, as well as harm and damage to its unwise and poor master builder.

Thus, without a given cause and reason or, at least, an apparent cause, did the Administration at Christiansborg Fortress dare to attack me again even though after its previous attack, it did not have much to do with me. Therefore I hoped, that I was certain of being dismissed from the service of the Company and therefore would not depend much on this Administration as it had not sent me in "black on white" or, as they say, "a written dismissal". There were several people in the Administration and at the Fortress amongst my secret, though at this point rather obvious, enemies who, in addition, were speculating about a large and subtle and therefore careful and cautious counsel and plot in order to catch and trap me.

This was a difficult plan to work out since they, most probably, realised that they were dealing with a subject who was cautious and who was, at this time, being most careful in his actions. They were almost bewildered and did not at all know any means or resort to trap me any more because in all my deeds and efforts, I had set up all

The *Theologian* Slave Trader

thinkable precautions to stop them from carrying out their evil intentions towards me, not merely for the present time but for the future, too. To my advantage, I had managed to acquire the applied for, and promised dismissal, though this had not yet been received in writing.

However, I did not think that the unsteady Governor Jurgensen would be so unsteady that in such a short time he would have changed his mind in order to deny what he had recently promised me, and deny me of my written document concerning my previously promised oral dismissal. I did not have, and could not imagine, any suspicion or thoughts about him. I had, for all likely situations, carefully provided myself with the manner of useful objections in order to prevent and hinder this and, amongst other obstacles which I assumed could meet me at this point in time. One such precaution was this: it was my intention to negotiate and sell my above-mentioned female slave at the first possible occasion, for the purpose of continuing my building work. This desired occasion arose quite conveniently and happened to me because a Frenchman had arrived from the roadstead – from a ship at the same place from where another Frenchman had recently arrived. Therefore, upon this message, I wanted to sell the aforementioned female slave. With her price and the value and sum of the goods, my building and hoped-for home could be brought to completion.

In order to negotiate the sale of this female slave on this ship, I applied for, and obtained from the Governor, permission and accept. Yet, I could not come on board the same day due to the strong surf on that day and I would have to await a change in the foaming surf. As the sea was not changing at Christiansborg Fortress during that day, I contemplated getting hold of a canoe from the Dutch bay and town or from a Negro settlement called Accra and to go on board. With the Governor's further permission and acceptance, I went there. However, when I arrived there, I encountered the same obstacles that forced me to return to Christiansborg Fortress with an unsolved course. In the case that I wanted to board the ship from the Dutch bay, I would have had to apply to the Dutch Governor, who had only been titled in this way for a few years, but otherwise was a Merchant, for permission. I would rather not do so, although I would have got the same permission from him as he had been my good friend, if I had requested one.

This passed on the Thursday before, being the third day prior to my painful and almost deadly arrest. Then on the second day, I changed my mind and decided to turn around and make my way to Teshi, a so-called Negro hamlet or town almost 2 miles from Christiansborg Fortress, to board the ship from that place but, before doing so, I was informed that the swell there was very severe with surfs more frothing and harmful than at Christiansborg Fortress so these reports kept me from going there.

[FREDERICUS IS ARRESTED AGAIN AND IMPRISONED]

I had prevented all possible predictable and likely obstacles with the largest and most imaginable precautions against problems, in the most careful way and down to minute detail, which I thought could meet me. Therefore, I had here, as the saying goes, "kept my eyes peeled" after sincere and serious admonitions from the next world which I had always endeavoured to observe and particularly so in those times after the many and varied occurred inconveniences in my life. It must sound to all Christians in general and directed to me at this time in particular: "You will be occupied by fear for as long as Your Abode is here".

On the Saturday, that is on the third day, after this waiting, the sea seemed somewhat calmer; it began to quieten down and settle a little but it had not yet become still so I dared not present myself on board the ship, which was still moored at the anchorage. Nevertheless, I assumed that that approaching night time the sea would have become so calm and quiet that I would be able to come on board in order to negotiate the sale of my female slave and, to this end, I had already ordered a canoe and a canoeist for this, or a black boatswain, who should transport me to the ship for a certain price according to a previously made accord.

The *Theologian* Slave Trader

But what happened? In the evening on the same day, as I returned home from my work hungry and tired and sat down at the table in the Negro hamlet in order to enjoy the nourishment and refreshment for this tired body which was a plain dish of beans, locally known as "round beans". But I had hardly got myself seated at the table before I saw a large number of Black people unexpectedly enter the small yard where I was sitting under the open sky for the refreshment for both body and soul. Quite contrary to their hopes, they saw and found me in the yard as they had otherwise expected to find and over power me in my room or in the house. With the greatest excitement after having approached me and, on the outside, greeted me very audibly by name and wished me a good evening, whereas in their minds they had prepared an entirely miserable evening for me. Following their verbal good wishes, they revealed their evil thoughts to me in that they attacked me without warning and with a united power and force tied me with a white cloth which they had brought with them. I thought it was indecent to tie me up with this cloth and far too fragile to keep me tied up. I immediately tore apart this cloth and I, single-handedly, drove these Negroes a little bit away. These Negroes were in total more than forty people.

When I had recovered a little, I quickly decided to surrender myself, considering at that moment that this expedition came from the Administration, all be it incognito. Although I certainly and reliably understood the craftiness, I stretched out my hands so they could tie them up, though I did think there was something contemptuous about this business. Then they began to tie me with my hands behind my back. What a slave-like way to tie up people! I confess that this was much more intolerable to me than the quite remarkable, impetuous and mad conduct that led to my arrest inside the Fortress Christiansborg, where I also saw that this was God's will according to His Majesty's miraculous and inscrutable counsel, just like a lamb being led to the slaughter house. I willingly let myself be taken by these delegates.

They were carefully instructed about their previous behaviour, words and deeds which apparently made the business more readily acceptable to them when they, amongst other things, said and announced that what they did, they did not do out of their own free will but that they had been sent there by the Governor. These words I merely registered for my information, everything that I demanded and needed for my information, not merely for the present time after these current circumstances, but just as much for the time to come due to any occurring and unexpected situations since these delegated, Black bandits had been commandeered to take me to the gates of the Fortress.

With diligence, these gates had been closed and the Black bandits then shouted to the sentry on duty, asking him to report to the Governor, who had been shooting outside in the evening at the Negro hamlet in the square next to the buildings which was not the thing to do, although the Governor at the Fortress could shoot day and night by use of the Fortress' and the Company's stocks and barrels of shooting equipments, at his own will and pleasure. I thought that I too, having been dismissed from the Company, even if by word and not yet in writing, and was therefore free and not depending on anybody, could also do so. Therefore, I too could take the liberty of taking some, if not to say or write, sodden pieces of old gun barrels to shoot and entertain myself with, for my pleasure and recreation. I did so and this led to my arrest.

Outside the gates of the Fortress I also asked these enchanted Negroes how they could be so daring and, without any polite ceremonies but in crude fashion, dared to catch and tie, indeed, the hands in a rather slave-like manner at the back of a free man even a respectable and previous Parish Clerk in the service of the Company who, in his time for ever and always, held conversations and company with the Governor, and had also had some degree of influence on the Administration, not merely so in the external affairs occurring from day to day in the Administration, but also in connection with the most private and secret posts from the Honourable Board themselves about which I had experience that they themselves could bear witness to, without any extensive search and scrutiny for other credible witnesses. Upon this, the most prominent amongst them and the Company's messenger and servant locally, Soya was his name, who was the most outstanding spokesman for the entire dispatched and commandeered conspiracy, answered the following way, on everybody's behalf, that they did not know if I was free of the Company's service. He then asked if I could produce my written, or put in their manner of speaking, not being proficient in the Danish language, or put rightly, a written resignation and dismissal from and by the Governor.

This trifle, I realised, they had been instructed about with great care, to make use of, in order to counter my rejections when necessary. I then answered, that I had not yet received the physical written dismissal which I had applied for and had been promised by the Governor, but was waiting for this, hoping that it would be convenient for the Governor to issue the dismissal tomorrow, provided this was not a Sunday.

While I was having this discussion with them, I was overcome by a terrible and dangerous impatience that strengthened my free resolve and un-tethered courage and heart that I, by stretching out my hands quickly once again, tore the cloth with which they had tied me up. When this happened, they burst out to me in these words, that they were under the Governor's order to catch me and tie me, therefore, they begged me that I should not blame them for this, as this was an issue which concerned, in their way of speaking, the White, and that, it was not for them to judge about the internal matters of the White. Now I had all the information I needed for my defence and intelligence for the future, concerning the actions which the Administration at Christiansborg had committed against me, be this immediately before an impartial Court set at Christiansborg Fortress or, at a later time or in eternity, if and when this may please God who alone and best knows my heart, as He is the only one who searches the heart's and the kidney's infallible, and the Board. Thank God, that I, on this day and time, might appear in the bright light of day for the investigation and its judgement.

In the meantime, the gates to the Fortress were opened up and I was forced inside after I had willingly offered my hands to them to let them be tied up. However, they showed themselves somewhat milder towards me than before as they tied my hands at the front. In this peculiar posture, I was now brought inside the Fortress, by the commandeer Negroes. I thought that according to custom and common practice in the country, I would have to report before the Governor, Mr Jurgensen, immediately that I had been taken prisoner, having been brought in, in this or that manner and for this or that reason. But I felt that I had been deceived about this, as without any of the aforementioned procedures, neither reporting to the Governor nor a complaint over why I was taken prisoner and led to the Fortress with my hands tied behind my back and then put into shackles - on feet and hands - like a slave or as some sort of serious offender or prisoner following Christiansborg's now thrice usual gesture and display of its peculiarly promised kindness and good, well-deserved attachment towards me.

Though this reward and these noble means with which to reward me for my great loyalty, honesty and sincerity towards Christiansborg Fortress and the entire Company and the affairs of the Honourable Board on the coast have not, in my opinion, corresponded to my well-deserving qualities, yet, what should the frail Parish Clerk, the hated Svane, the right and justice, the honesty and sincerity, the obedient humility, and Svane with his lovingly sworn faithfulness, then resort to? When power comes before justice, when deceitfulness like "James" (in the Christian Bible) is kissing the innocent like the pious "Abner Ner's son" (in the Christian Bible) in the next world; when unfaithfulness is holding the seat of justice, then there is no remedy, justice or truth. I walked upright through the gate, walking without bending though only for some time. The time for refreshment from the face of the Lord will come sometime. This, I must acknowledge according to my modest intellect and few years of age, to Your Excellency and the Honourable Gracious Gentlemen Directors, to have learnt from the wise teacher, virtuous, experienced and reasonably skilled in this native language and speech.

There was nothing to be done. Like the old student proverb "Molens Volens": "Whether wanting to or not", I had to go wherever I was taken and, in this way, my next destination and temporary lodgings became the "Black Hole". This incarceration treatment and referral to free lodging could now, as well as previously, have been my room at Christiansborg Fortress and it did not take place with any kind of politeness or courtesy, nor with the conduct or treatment which would be used towards a respectable person or a decent prisoner who could, depending on the nature of the case, be pardoned in due time and be released again.

Instead, I was treated like the most rude evildoer and murderer who could have killed his father and mother and where no rescue could be envisaged for the future life according to any fair law or finding. Worst of all, this happened on a Saturday evening before a Sunday, when I should and ought to gather my thoughts and prayers in preparation seemingly for Christ prior to the approaching Sabbath and day of rest. Yet, such matters did not enjoy much respect at Christiansborg and, least of all, at this point in time, as justice died at Christiansborg Fortress with the death of Schielderup. Moreover, his stepsister was also put away with their forefathers and this monstrous creature Boris and lowly elder son of "Nabil" (in the Christian Bible) and his brothers with him governed the Fortress of the Honourable Company.

With the greatest pain to both body and mind, I had to spend this night sitting down. On the morning after, which was Sunday, I had hardly any calm in my body and mind and could therefore manage only a poor prayer which was nevertheless seemly for a holy day such as this. Still, on the evening before, I had imagined for certain, that I would definitely be taken out from there and relieved of my shackles as I was assuredly thinking that my service in the church as a Parish Clerk and Cantor would necessarily have to be carried out and so they would have to remove and free me from my heavy shackles so that I could attend to this business as I had not yet received my dismissal in writing from the service as Parish Clerk at the Fortress Christiansborg.

[FREDERICUS DESCRIBES THE EFFECTS OF ALCOHOLIC DRINKS FROM CHRISTIANSBORG ON THE LOCAL VILLAGERS]

Thus passed also this day for me in my black cell, the "Black Hole". During the following night, between Sunday and Monday, I was overcome by an overwhelmingly strong impatience because of the poor bed and my low spirits due to my poor fate and the unreasonable, evil, unlawful, and rather inhuman, very cruel and harsh treatment, amongst other evil which I had to endure. For example, the bandit-like assault and attack by the Blacks who had been commandeered, being Governor Jurgensen's assistants, and several of the assistants to persons in the important ranks at Christiansborg Fortress and also a few young Negroes from the Negro hamlet, possibly acting under orders from Governor Jurgensen or Monsieur Blass, either for a glass of distilled spirits or some such a thing since they had themselves a strong affection for this as their best nectar and heavenly drink be it night or day, which was thus agreed and given. One should not be surprised that such a lowly gift of strong drink of liquid, could produce this kind of good-will and service from these blind heathens who lived without any conscience or without any part in God's true gifts.

The Negroes in Africa and on the Coast of Guinea in particular, and especially so at Accra and around there, were such blind heathens that they worshipped sticks and stones, lumps of clay and soil painted red and white, wood and bones, drums and threads with oil from palm nuts which were taken to paint red for their dead people's funeral celebrations. These imagined symbols of holiness were worn round their necks, on their legs, around their loins, in their hair, hanging from their heads, occasionally with white corals for peculiar adornment and "Zirath", an ornament of important sacredness and splendour. Indeed, they worshipped even the things most unnatural that are incarnate contrary to all common sense and natural light in the most contradictory and unreasonable ways. For example, respectfully referring to Your Excellency and all the Gracious Gentlemen Directors, in their gracious presence, so dirty and lowly that to mention this is almost disrespectful: such as cow dung, several year old heads of humans and cattle, and their brows, and legs, teeth and bones and much more of a similar kind, which is not necessary to elaborate on here and should be passed over.

The above mentioned, such as this my most humble description on these few pages regarding the circumstances on the coast during my time, for Your Excellency, following Your Excellency's gracious order to me, I present herewith, my most humble and truthful general account and declaration's content, not particularly graceful, for example, this material concerning the heathenism in Africa and, in particular, on the Coast of Guinea, at the part called Accra, which is my dear native land. Such malaises should, most of all, be treated on their own as they could lead to a rather elaborate opus and, with these few words I have therefore, not attempted to do so. In as much as the natural condition and the current affairs of these Negroes are concerned, they are as blind a people as can be found in this world, and, of all stories, one can hardly read of a more stupid people under the course of the blessed sun and perpetual daily course at the great Fortress, and the Heavens could hardly be presented a more blind, indeed and in one word, more foolish nation than these people in my so very dear, native land.

However, returning to my eventful account and purpose, it cannot cause much surprise that these simple Negroes, these mad heathens, without a God and a Christ, alien to the Testament of the Promises and therefore also without any conscience could let themselves be persuaded and induced to carry out and commit towards me the acts which they perpetrated against me here at that time and, least of all, one should not be surprised that to commit this towards me here, they have simply let themselves be bought for distilled spirits when they, with the same reward, could as often happens here on the coast, be bought to commit murder on their own kind. Indeed even more than that, sometimes they commit murder on their own close family members and those related to them through blood.

The latter is a strangely miserable incident that took place during the last days while I was still at the Fortress on the coast only a very short time prior to our sailing from the country. Please note: "Cabuser" is the chief in each town or Negro settlement. Pulli, the Cabuser in Labadi, now also a Negro hamlet, trading with the main Fortress Christiansborg, was rather an elderly and strangely intelligent person who was loyal, benign and sincere towards the Company. A well-known man in that country who enjoyed great respect for his sincerity and, for a heathen, he had an unusually great intelligence and many years of experience.

Until my next and final departure from Africa and the Coast of Guinea, I was staying in this Negro hamlet as guest of this man on my miserable escape from Christiansborg Fortress. Pulli's own brother, namely Qvasi, was a very honest and wise Negro, though only poor, and he was my brother and Sergeant at arms at Fredensborg Fortress, Johan Ditlev's father-in-law. He was a Negro who particularly when I first arrived there, to the hamlet of Labadi, tried hard to be at my service in every possible way and in all possible matters. Amongst other things, he made himself available to work for me in strangely advantageous ways in the future though only, for a start, for the sake of the initial costs, merely a seemingly moderately advantageous service, namely this man urged of his own initiative, offered himself as the first proof of his special helpfulness and good affection towards me. As I was already in Labadi, his native Negro hamlet and his inheritance, as the next in line after the death of his brother Cabuser Pulli in Labadi, he asked if I could get him some small goods to negotiate for me so that the value would be enough for him to acquire a female slave and, if not, a full adult male slave, or a mediocre slave-boy, for me, in order that I could have some help or advantage when trading my own necessary provisions there in that town and country.

This was so because he and many others, indeed most people in the hamlet of Labadi, felt great kindness towards me, Svane, the former Parish Clerk at the Fortress Christiansborg, who was now disowned from the Fortress, hated and fleeing Svane in Labadi. As they all saw me in this town, and being Negroes, in my present great lack of necessary articles, even the most basic items for life's keep, they thought that I ought to have a little bit means with which to earn and procure my daily food.

All the Negroes in this Negro hamlet agreed in their hearts to help me though I must acknowledge, and I was aware, that the same Negroes were a very poor yet considerate people, diligently working the land in order to cultivate crops at the right time each year and they did therefore, have a special commiseration with me, particularly so during this my final time in that country and my escape from it, as everyone of them displayed to me all the natural politeness, service, loyalty and sincerity. Yes, even by way of lending me a free house for as long as I was staying with them because I had nothing left to pay with.

The *Theologian* Slave Trader

What compassion and commiseration, loyalty and sincerity, honesty and helpfulness in, and even from, these heathens here enabled me on my dangerous and poor escape to experience the enjoyment of tranquillity for some time and after many miserable years of toilsome service at the Fortress of Christiansborg, for the refreshment and recreation of the mind in the company of these faithful and honest Negroes in this town. Yet, what happened? The above mentioned Cabuser Pulli's brother, Qvasi, and heir after him, as well as Qvasi being my brother's father-in-law, and towards me being a very forthcoming and helpful person, Qvasi acquired, after well-intended demand of me, some advantageous gains to seek for him and I. Therefore, Qvasi acquired some commodities after the coast's price in order to sell and be able to buy the said male or a female slave for me. However, this was only a very slight advantage to me, but a great harm to himself and his brother, as well as the most regrettable tragedy in the entire town and Negro hamlet of Labadi. As, when undertaking the journey to his planned purpose and place, he was unexpectedly assaulted and killed by his own sister's son, Tay.

In that country rumours had it that he, namely Tay, now the mediator or spokesman for the negotiators at Fredensborg Fortress at Ningo, had hired a male slave to commit that crime. Although this Negro Tay said he did not commit the awful murder of his own mother's brother Qvasi with his own two hands, he had still, according to widespread rumours, bought a Black Sharpshooter for this purpose and it was supposed to be for just one or a couple of bottles of distilled spirits along with other things which he had promised to a bought Negro slave, in return for this unheard of deed of murder of his uncle. Although it is the case that these Negroes on the Coast of Guinea possess such a brutality, however, according to this truthful account and event, even though heathens, these acts were done only by some of them, as it would certainly not be good if they were all in this way inclined; the most simple people under the sun, without any kind of conscience, can let themselves be bought for such a murderous act with a bottle of distilled alcoholic spirits.

[FREDERICUS CONTINUES TO DESCRIBE HIS SECOND ARREST]

Thus, it was much less surprising that Governor Jurgensen and Bookkeeper Blass had been able to order these delegates to assault, capture, take me prisoner and to lead me tied up to the Fortress and the Administration purely, as it has been mentioned, for some bottles of spirits. Still, amongst all the other things that I had to endure during that evening, I shall now turn my pen and my thoughts from the very case as hitherto described in the above and which has taken place at this point if not that all of its events and circumstances have been described, to my own circumstances in the "Black Hole". This was not right, even to the meanest, that I only had little food and soon no food. Indeed, on the day I was captured, on that occasion, I was torn away from the table by the Black bandits. On the following Sunday, I only got little food, too. Therefore, in the night that followed, I could not do anything but feel hungry and thirsty as on this day the heat was very penetrating.

With my mind being so strongly affected by the hostility, I finally broke the irons one more time after I had broken them the first time in the previous gaol that was supposed to be a civil gaol. As I had now torn apart the irons and tough shackles, I thought that I would no longer let myself be held captive in this bad hole, this foul and ugly gaol in the Fortress, especially as I was innocent and without the slightest cause for blame given to me as well as, and without, even the slightest allegation about any matter. If only such an allegation could be disputable whether this was either to conform, in accordance with the truth and fairness or not, legal or illegal, valid or reprehensible, arising from an actually committed misdeed or from any kind of unlawful fabrication and persecution aimed at the suspected offender, either denunciation or a mitigation of the sentence, or even at closer impartial investigation of the above mentioned unfairly accused sinner's absolute release and finding from the attributed case depending on the true and legal nature of the case.

The *Theologian* Slave Trader

From the judge, or from the superiors who were under orders for this purpose by the high authorities after the clear and holy God's law and the common sense of nature and all just laws with one origin, the great God, its content found to be fair and right, ought to be presented when the court should have its just cause. That the judges or the authorities could defend, enforce and maintain the name of a wise and upright judge and authority and that, in the meantime, could make it possible for the benefit of the sinners to attend, in some way or other, to some kind of enlightenment, in order to discover the case and its nature. The sentence could be accommodated and based on this before it could or would come to any extreme action towards the offenders. However, this in my humble opinion is a lawful approach to pleading, but no one had yet cared to support me at Christiansborg Fortress, as far as my case was concerned neither were they familiar with this procedure. Such ignorance, which was here undoubtedly, the true cause for my unlawful imprisonment, could have driven me even to death itself, for this evil thoughtless urge to deal with me in the obviously most unfair and irresponsible extreme manner. More will follow hereafter.

However, in this prosecution taken by Mr Jurgensen and the Administration against me no questions were posed about the case, the guilt or the offence in even the slightest way, as far as I am aware. When I, as mentioned, had broken the irons because of my overwhelming impatience and thus had freed myself from this burden and coercion, I was now free and I also wanted to get out to go under the free and open sky, but there did not seem to be any opportunity for me. I saw that I was incarcerated in a strong prison cell which was just as strong as it was ugly and awful and so it was not easy for me to get out of there. Yet, what may not be achieved by impatience, when violence and premeditated cruelty and tyranny take over against an innocent person? Foolishness and wickedness take power over the powerless and frail Parish Clerk. As the saying goes:

"When gratitude from poor insight and nature is for his loyal service, sincerity and unadulterated honesty rewarded with ingratitude's coin and currency, then it is no mystery that he stands up with impatience and the people who have carried out good deeds can only regret this which has so badly lost its well-meaning kindness and benefaction and search for his own safety when a very innocent person is ill-treated contrary to all he deserves". This also happened to me in the cell here at Christiansborg.

Having freed myself from the shackles and achieved the freedom of the body, I knocked a hole in the wall at the door to my dark cell in the hope that I could reach freedom from the severe coercion which I did not see any hopes of escaping from other than by my own efforts which probably could not be regarded as unfair since I, as innocent, could not see any useful or advantageous occasion and I was in particular driven to this by a rumour that I had received on Sunday about the Governor's harder and more unjust ill-treatment for me on one of the coming days, thereafter as they would weigh me down with an incredible amount of iron so that it would be reasonable to conclude that nothing else would follow but my certain death.

I was overcome by great impatience because of the serious harm, shame and damage that I had to suffer though innocent. I was also affected by the fabricated suspicion and harsh handling of me by the Administration to which, God is my best and only witness, followed by themselves and their own conscience. Finally, people on the entire coast and in the surroundings of our Danish Fortress, as well as our trading partners, in particular, at Accra on the Guinea Coast, Blacks as well as Whites, all knew that I was innocent. How much good I had deserved from the Administration at Christiansborg Fortress during all my time in my service there, that I never got. Indeed I dare to say and announce this with a clean conscience before God and the entire world, that I served as a loyal and sincere, upright and enterprising servant in the lawful and respectable Company's service. Not merely in my given position but even in all arising occasions, with this and that, served this or that task according to the necessary circumstances in every situation, always considering my perpetual and humble commitment towards the Board.

I had always worked with delight and diligence, paid attention to, and fulfilled a task for the sake of the purpose of it. To this, I can and will say with a clean conscience like "Job" to God's law and honour:

The *Theologian* Slave Trader

"My witness be in the Heavens and he who knows me well is in the Heavens!" Oh yet, why present these high and precious challenges? After all, when I consider my duty with regards to the honourable Board, my limited years of gracious care and training by the Board, several years of devout care and maintenance of academic subjects and the same Christian care's gracious continuation here at the Royal Academy for some years by the help of the Honourable Board for a Christian purpose, then, I have to confess that no matter how great a service I had given there, my humble duty and commitment should have been yet bigger in displaying my gratitude for the Honourable Board's good deed towards me. Although I have always dedicated myself to the duty of the Company with all my heart, with all my efforts, I must still before the sight of God, consider my own lowly person and ineptitude full of shortcomings and much frailty and confess that never have I worked so much that I ought not have worked harder still. The Lord is my true witness and only judge against all my enemies at Christiansborg Fortress and before his countenance I stand. All this notwithstanding, it was the case that I had to bend my weak shoulders under the yoke, my poor body under the bolt and iron, much so at present but much more so in the time to come.

I can never describe sufficiently and with the pen portray the state of incredible fear and pain of my poor heart throughout this night especially when I heard for certain the reliable information about how much evil the Administration had in store for me at Christiansborg Fortress, at this time. I could literally see and feel with my bare hands, in accordance with God's inscrutable ways, that the Devil had hidden secret reasons and had decided this time to subject me, God's most lowly servant, to them, to worm and maggot. All the Devil's cruelty and wrath! However, whilst I had torn myself lose, I had destroyed so much of the wall at the door in this bad cell that I could easily get out and free myself of this miserable state and, in this way, avoid the approaching quite inhuman, undeserved and irresponsible behaviour towards me from those who had promised me so much kindness. Everybody who knew me on the Coast, Europeans as well as Africans, Whites as well as Blacks, knew and acknowledged, that I had always served, sometimes even to my own harm, with night duties and long hours on alert, with my own humble yet useful advice for the common good and purpose according to the talents and gift of grace that my God has entrusted to me. It was also known that I had thus made the most of these talents following the example of the kind and diligent servant I was, such as by enduring dangers at sea, when I not only once but often and several times had been running with my life in my hands between the tiresome and quibbling Governor and his Council to establish appeasement, reconciliation and creation of friendship between them in order to achieve agreement, trust and good understanding.

Here, none of these were of any help to the poor incarcerated Parish Clerk, the honest and upright Svane. It was now the will of God that at this time and place, I should be subjected to suffering, imprisonment and chains. I realised this and so by prayer and supplication to God, I endeavoured to endure and bear this ordeal more readily the longer it went on, still assuming that the God who had let them place this burden on me should also help me carry this burden. For this reason I, though I could probably have avoided the approaching great suffering and the distress, the anguish and the future's burden of serious misery, stayed yet inside in silence and calm during that night and the following day, though without irons and shackles, under a very heavy guard of mostly Blacks, namely the Company's slaves and the Governor's guards.

But on the following Tuesday, the sad act took place and then Satan's lock and lot became obvious in its wrath and bitterness, its tyrannous cruelty, barbaric harshness, its severe evilness, and hate towards an innocent and honest person. Then, without any given explanation and with a handling which is not lawful in even the slightest way and, quite unlawful in its unjust and cruel treatment, as for the coarsest and most aggressive culprit and murderer, I was covered in so much iron and shackles and an incredible amount of chains on the hands and feet as is hardly imaginable to a mortal human being; a most cruel way in which to pester and torment the most guilty and horrible brutes let alone another human being who has the same and not a more robust nature than himself, who owns a heart no harder than his own, who is dressed in the same kind of frail flesh and blood as himself. Oh, what inhuman cruelty! Oh, what awful harshness!

This very regrettable, shameful, rather ridiculous, miserable and spectacular deed; Christiansborg had never previously seen before in the ordinary, low and common custody cell, the "Black Hole", thus called because of its foulness and darkness. Before this took place, I say, concerning the executed pathetic and regrettable act, the gates to Christiansborg Fortress were closed and parades of soldiers were put in place. The shackles were then produced together with various strange, peculiar and numerous ways to put them into place to burden a frail and humble human being and prisoner, as if he had killed both his father and mother or committed the most serious and brutal crime. This was done to disgrace me.

The purpose was to fulfil the goal and purpose of Christiansborg Fortress, with its greed and inhuman cruelty and barbarism: namely my hurt and much tormented mind's very painful feeling from this Administration's currently inflicted brutality, cruelty and harm. This was meant to take out its most bitter gall on me who was bent so deeply to the ground with the most venomous words from this inhumanly hard, destructive heart inside Monsieur Blass, the Bookkeeper. This was for his own pleasure and he was happy to carry out the execution of this act against an innocent person and, to the scrupulous and most responsible descendants, this action was pathetic done by him and the Governor, the most merciless people seen in the world at this time.

While Monsieur Blass satisfied his hateful and cruel lion eyes, he exclaimed these heart-hurting words in the most, bitter tongue, in order to increase my disgrace, spite and great pain, and said to me:

> *"Now, consider this beautiful suit, Svane, and make sure you do your best to break free of these too. But I hope you will not do it. If you can, then do it better!"*

Oh! What painful, distressing and heartless words! But what could I do? The pious "Mother Patience" was comforting me in my woe from this great pain and commanded me secretly in my heart to listen to this and to tolerate it as much as everything else at this time in my life for great trials.

Thus, Gracious Master, Your Excellency and all Honourable Gentlemen Directors, my back was weighted down and burdened with iron. At the front, I was so tied up and covered that from the shackles at the feet a chain went to both hands, also the hand shackles forced both hands with an equally thick iron bolt and the shackles around each hand were attached to this chain from the feet.

In addition to this strong hand shackle, which was also shaped with the greatest precision, there extended yet another one chain of forged iron of equal thickness and strength right over to my left side where the biggest weight on the Fortress was standing. It was used for weighing elephant tusks. Moreover, one long and strong iron chain that completed the whole work was going from the hand shackle to the neck placing heaviness and burden on my poor body. Finally, from the shackles around the feet a very strong chain also led straight to an extremely large pine beam that was conveniently placed or brought in with diligence in the moment my arrest was announced and left in place during my coming half year in custody. To this beam an exceedingly strong chain with a great thickness and strength equal to an iron bolt, was fastened with a hammer. This beam was the thickest and strongest in the entire Fortress and, length wise it was nearly 4 meters long and 5 1/2 meters in diameter thickness.

With this heavy burden and inhuman heaviness I was, Your Excellency and all of the Honourable Gentlemen Directors, nailed to the ground and had to lie there for an entire half year in Christiansborg Fortress dungeon. From this, it was very easy to establish the murderous intentions of the good Administration, namely my final death and destruction.

[FREDERICUS'S BELONGINGS ARE AUCTIONED AND THE FOUNDATION OF HIS BUILDING DESTROYED]

On the Monday following my arrest, all of my modest property was packed into a large chest of mine. According to my calculations, the property amounted to a sum of 362 Rdl. or more. Although I had to

The *Theologian* Slave Trader

be without many of my things, this chest was brought to, and placed outside the door to my cell. Here, everything that I owned was auctioned before my eyes to my further pain and hurt, yet I remained still and took my pleasure in seeing these men competing for my belongings and grabbing them like roaring lions. The most painful thing was to witness that they sold most of the items for hardly anything. Amongst some of my belongings there were things which I had recently purchased for 6 Rdl. that were being sold for five "skilling". A "Skilling" is a small fraction of the value of one Rdl.- "Rigsdaler". I would have liked to bid too, but this was not allowed. When they wanted to bid amongst themselves, especially the military functionaries, one more than the other as done in the common tradition at auctions, the Governor forbade this and said in public that they ought to consider their stomachs.

While enjoying the process of this public auction event, Governor Jurgensen also enjoyed a glass of spirits which functionaries, who were still alive and amongst us, and the subordinates at the Fortress, indeed, his own conscience as well as Whites and Blacks, could witness. I, poor captive and innocent man, had to witness this event which had not been subjected to any law, with a silence which was rather hurting, without any witnesses and without any final judgement under pretext that what took place there happened in order to pay my debt, although in my good conscience I did not owe anybody except Governor Jurgensen to whom I owed 24 Rdl. in gold and 80 Rdl., which in Bosh, the local currency, amounted in total to the sum of 64 Rdl. in gold. I was in fact some time previously given 2 slaves by the Governor, namely 2 male slaves in kind, of whom I wanted to negotiate the sale of one and I did also have this same slave here already traded away, as mentioned here in this my humble work, to the French ship at the mooring, off the Fortress Christiansborg at Accra. The other slave, I still owed Mr Jurgensen for, namely, in the previous case he released a male slave, a brother of the first slave, whom I had with me for my work in order to help with my building. Moreover, some months before, I had also procured some goods from Mr Jurgensen that had to be paid for with a fine female slave. In total this amounted to 3 slaves; 2 men and 1 female, whom I owed the Governor. Yet, at my arrest, Mr Jurgensen also put my 3 slaves in shackles, possibly, I thought, to secure the 3 slaves who were owed to him, in order that they should know that they were his slaves.

Amongst my own previously owned male slaves, at least one was still on the Coast, under the Fortress in the slave dungeons and in the service of the Company, at the time I left Christiansborg Fortress, so I therefore hoped to be absolutely blameless from the Governor's demands for these three slaves. Governor Jurgensen had not yet satisfied his greed. On the following day, which was a Tuesday, he ordered all Negro males and females to destroy the foundation of my building which was fairly advanced and to take away all the stones which had been collected in many heaps for the building at an extraordinarily high cost and at great trouble and, without any further consideration, Mr Jurgensen then let aprons be built and repaired at Christiansborg Fortress with these materials, regardless that the Governor was not unaware of how considerable the costs of the great diligence and labour which had been spent on this, which Your Excellency and Honourable Gentlemen Directors will most graciously have learned from the previous account and see that this had not been a modest sum.

In short, in this way did not only my long effort and labour soon get ruined, in addition, at least an amount of 800 Rdl. was wasted besides what my possessions could have yielded from a proper and free bidding at a public auction. This and other matters I report for Your Excellency and the Honourable Gentlemen Directors' most gracious comments. During my time in the cell and in custody, I did not have anything but water and bread and, for company, I had rats and mice and other of the country's unpleasant creatures. Nobody was allowed to speak to me. When in my misery, I supplicated God with song and reading, Cornelius Petersen, the Sergeant at Arms, who was outside my cell door, once said that I was calling for the Devil whose evil spirit, he said, I was consulting for help and advice in my hour of need.

The *Theologian* Slave Trader

The permitted bread that came with the water was so strictly controlled that when I, with permission and for the sake of my health, had my own bread prepared by my niece, a Mulatto woman by the name Helena, it was broken into pieces by orders and, when they found any meat in it, this was taken out and the pieces were then given to me. They let two bundles of sticks be carried to my cell door for me to be beaten with but I said that such things should be used on a boy but not I who was a grown man and, if I really was to be beaten, then iron bars would be appropriate for me. Twice I tore myself loose from all the iron and I was then brought into the yard as a spectacle and burdened with sturdy, unbreakable iron chains and bars.

When I later came into the foul cell, the door outside was barred with two large iron bars and a guard was barring the area outside the gaol during the day but at night the ordinary guard on the battery on each hour and each stroke of the bell came down together with the patrolling petty officer to inquire if somebody was going to, or had dared to, try to work on the heavy lock in order to open the door and give me my freedom. They gave a few of my old shirts back to me in the gaol, but I almost had to tear them apart because of all the iron that they had to accommodate on my body and these shirts were almost dissolved through to my skin because of the rust from the iron. In this way I had to cope by myself until the merchant at Ningo Fredensborg Fortress, Christen Glob Dorph, became Governor; that happened the following way.

Satan and his kingdom became divided, as the Bookkeeper Monsieur Blass began a new strife with the Governor whose soft temperament and weak and effeminate nature he, Blass, began to challenge and also to provoke such an effeminacy, more and more as the days went past, which was not proper for him the Governor, to receive and to tolerate. Yet, being an effeminate person, he had to endure the Bookkeeper's frequent acts of coarseness which were committed in his drunkenness until this came to extremes where the Bookkeeper even pursued Jurgensen into his own hall with a drawn sword at hand, as I was told in gaol, in order to stab the Governor to death.

The constant fear of, and danger from, the Bookkeeper Blass and his drawn sword finally made it necessary for the former Governor, Jurgensen, to resort to Mr Christen Glob Dorph for help, to solve his daily calamities, imploring him for advice and remedy for this. Upon this, Dorph who had often previously been a reconciler between these two clashing parties, finally became tired and weary of these predictable daily journeys to create reconciliation between them and, in order to save money on costs which had to be spent on this matter, he resorted to a resolution with the Governor, to come to an agreement with the Administration. This came to a desirable end for Mr Jurgensen who resigned and handed the Administration to the merchant Christen Glob Dorph in May, in the year of 1743, after having made and drawn up a written agreement for his pleasure and safety. Approximately a fortnight after he had taken over the Administration, Mr Dorph spoke with me in my hitherto difficult cell. More about this will follow. The period during the rule of this much described Governor Jurgensen, from the death and burial of his predecessor, Mr Boriss on the 21st of June 1740 until 29th of May 1743, was 3 years bar 17 days.

[FREDERICUS IS RELEASED AS GLOB DORPH IS SWORN IN AS THE NEW GOVERNOR]

>Honourable Mr Christen Glob Dorph
>Governor And Colony Manager
>At The Fortress Christiansborg;
>His Accession To The Administration,
>His Progress In The Administration,
>His Final Resignation That Took Place
>On The 2nd Of February 1744.

When the former Governor, Mr Jurgensen, driven by pressing reasons that were acknowledged by him and known to everybody else, had resigned after previous written agreement drawn up between him and Mr Dorph, Mr Christen Glob Dorph finally took over the Administration as the Governor. His first concern at the

The *Theologian* Slave Trader

commencement of his rule, amongst other things, was to consider how to bring reasonable good order to the Administration that had been left in a certainly great disorder by his good predecessor. His industrious efforts also became directed at my person in order to bring an end to resolve the subsequent difficulties following my imprisonment. Upon this, the new Governor decided to send down to me in the cell the new already changed Council in the Administration, consisting of the following: Simon H. Klein, Ludvig Ferdinand Romer and Lauritz Bay, with the following proposal from the Governor. That the Governor, Mr Christen Glob Dorph, together with the entire Secret Privy-Council had, on the new change in the Administration amongst other matters, also ventilated about my person and the occurred and existing considerable difficult case.

Upon this they had resolved to do what was found to be right, and make a change for me to obtain my freedom and my former position and in order to restore all matters to good order provided I would forget this supposed injustice and all the revenge which I could in the future bring it up as an accusation, and state any strange disadvantage and responsibility for the former Governor Jurgensen and his Administration. This meant that, I had to forget about the problems I had with the previous Administration and let it die in my mind. Moreover, I was required to lead a life which was inoffensive hereafter and in the future in my restored work and position, which should correspond to the life I had led previously in suitably respectable circumstances which I had had prior to this disturbing disorder.

They pointed out to me on behalf of the Governor, that if the new Administration could be assured of this, then they assured me on behalf of everybody, that everything would be restored for me over time. And I, immediately upon such reassurance about my taken resolution and the Governor's towards me, as well as his previously well-known favour towards me while he was in charge as a merchant on Fredensborg Fortress, and his future kind favour towards me hereafter now as Governor at Christiansborg, which they assured me about, to this assurance on behalf of the Governor and the entire recently established Council, I also gave my final resolution and necessary declaration.

Following this, I was released from my burden and harsh gaol, and I was then taken up to the Governor's hall where I found both Governors, the previous Governor Mr Jurgensen, and Mr Christen Glob Dorph, the present Governor and the Secret Privy-Council, both the old and the new as well as all the Company's subordinate functionaries from the highest ranking to the lowest ranking, all gathered and placed after rank and dignity.

There, all these posts were proposed and I declared all for my friends. In addition, committed on my side, that all things should rest on the above mentioned conditions and to my, in the previous Administration unfairly executed treatment and harm and ruin. Thus, over time and with Mr Dorph's promised and reliable goodwill, restitution and such expressed initiatives that would also be necessary for my precaution in the future were also ventilated, deliberated and discussed so that nobody hereafter in the service of the entire Company should or could dare to display any hostility towards me as to what had happened previously. In this way, things took place with the Whites. Afterwards, the highest ranking amongst the Negro and White subordinates at the Fortress, amongst whom all the Blacks or Negroes at the Fortress who depended on the Administration for its justice, were called into the same honourable gathering so that I also on my part, could declare to them, that all of them were my friends and that I did not hold against any of them what they had done and committed against me.

[FREDERICUS WRITES ABOUT THE DISMISSAL OF GOVERNOR DORPH]

This new elected and accepted Governor, Christen Glob Dorph, was previously a merchant at the Fortress and defences Fredensborg at Ningo. He was a competent individual in the service of the Company on the coast as regards his experiences about all aspects of trading activities on the coast, which were proper for such a person as well as for the affairs of the Company and the Administration. He was well suited in all respects; courteous and well-liked by all of the foreign European nations present on that Coast. He was quick witted and

The *Theologian* Slave Trader

quick at adjusting himself to new customs. He was kind-hearted towards everybody and fairly strict with the administration of the laws. He was sympathetic and quite passionate. In fact, to put it short, he was a God's son. Eventually, he was dismissed and replaced by the Honourable Jurgen Billsen who became his successor.

Nota bene!

The Honourable Mr Christen Glob Dorph was of an exceedingly reasonable nature to his own great harm and to the great disadvantage to both himself and to the Honourable Company. His rise from Managing Clerk to the advantageous management of high affairs and important office as a Governor, was too much for him. He probably did not consider carefully or really plan at the time of Mr Jurgensen's resignation, to undertake a position such as one of an important description requiring necessarily and indispensably clear and proper accounts of the trusted goods which he ought to have carried out when signing an agreement to take over from Governor Jurgensen.

According to my modest thoughts, Mr Dorph should have considered somewhat more carefully and not just proceed so blindly without having made the necessary reflection concerning the right accounts of the Administration in the future, when it might please the Honourable Board most graciously to think otherwise if they so pleased and to arrange a new and different Governor for the Fortress and the Administration. This did in fact happen, although, this was possibly not anticipated by Mr. Dorph, as Governor Mr Billsen's new appointment, was made by the Honourable Board in Copenhagen. If Mr. Dorph, a Merchant, had earlier thought this over thoroughly and wisely, contemplated and planned beforehand, then he would, perhaps, not have run for this appointment without precise calculation, to receive Mr Jurgensen's Administration, which was found to be in a state of the greatest disorder and confusion.

The ensuing situation was quite fatal and alarming for Mr Billsen and was of poor advantage and gain also for the Honourable Company. I do not know how this had happened and therefore cannot give any further information. But I had known this situation from himself, as I knew also from other sources, as I had always been told by Mr Billsen and, in addition, I knew from the Private and Secrecy Post and recondite knowledge about Mr Dorph's established incorrect and large defect in the handing over of the accounts in addition to the assumed complicated Administration, which came to light after his predecessor was taking over, namely a defect of 8 thousand Rdl. This large sum might, in due course, have to be compensated to the Honourable Board in the following manner: Mr Christen Glob Dorph had considerable outstanding debts on the Coast which, as far as was known to me, these debts concerned Negroes who were always willing to work for him on credit. The Company's messenger in the country at that time was called Soya. He could give the most well informed information about this matter, as it was customary in such cases, in accordance with the nature of his service and duty, to demand the amount, or seize his possessions, if the Gracious Gentleman decided to protest against this debt, as the amount had to be paid down to the last "skilling", which is a fraction of the Rdl.

However, Dorph's goods were released since the above mentioned debts had not taken place as an embezzlement, neither now nor before after Dorph's replacement and departure from the coast like the several succeeding Governors and the "ad interims". It was known on the Coast that Dorph in his case, because of his established incorrect housekeeping, fell into disfavour with the Honourable Gentleman Governor Jurgen Billsen on his arrival, and therefore, the Honourable Gentleman was no more in the service of the Company. Hopefully, he had been promoted. The aforementioned Governor Dorph was in charge for this period of time: 8 months and 4 days, namely from 29th May 1743 until 2nd February, the year of 1744.

Furthermore, the Honourable Christen Glob Dorph was also found to be in such diffuse circumstances concerning the accounts in relation to the replacement that he even, in addition, and on behalf of the Honourable Company, run up a considerable debt of 4 thousand Rdl approximately which, if not cleared, was a serious situation as was known to me. This debt was incurred for necessary assistance, presumably for the necessary maintenance of the Fortress and the trade on behalf of the Company by Mr Christen Dorph with the English Nation's representation on the Coast there, with their then trusted Head Clerk at their James Fortress, at Accra, by orders. This trusted Head Clerk, Mr. Dithmar, was also a Merchant.

The *Theologian* Slave Trader

[FREDERICUS WRITES ABOUT JURGEN BILLSEN'S GOVERNORSHIP]

Honourable Mr Jurgen Billsen,
Governor And Colony Manager On The Fortress Christiansborg
His Arrival To The Coast And Fortress, Administration And Rule,
Curiously Occurring Adventurer And Eventually,
Strange Death And Departure From This World, etc.

Following the previous Governor "ad interim" Christen Glob Dorph, the succeeding honourable Billsen was sent to the Coast by the Board in Copenhagen to be the new Governor. He was a man typical of his age and time, and he possessed a natural competence, who seemed set for great things if only he could find honest and loyal subjects before him in the Administration. This could have helped him to acquire the necessary information on the Coast, with respects to the trade and correspondence, in addition to other highly required necessities which were not only warranted from such a man but was also proper for a person of his high ranking.

But the damage was that, in his mind, he found a Council that respected him less than they promised him on his arrival and commencement in the Administration, with respect to the affairs of the Company and the information about the situation on the Coast. According to his own confession to me while he was still alive he had, in the beginning, for Monsieur Simon H. Klein, formerly Merchant at Ningo, yet only "ad interim" but now with Billsen's Governorship, given the authority and power of attorney from the Secret Privy-Council. Billsen also licensed the actual Merchant and Manager's position at the Fortress and defences at Fredensborg Fortress to Ludvig Ferdinand Romer as Head-Assistant. And also during the term and rule of Mr Jurgensen, Bookkeeper Blass was an Assistant and Helper in the office and continued afterwards, during the term and rule of Mr Christen Glob Dorph, was also used as mediator and interpreter for the French trading ships, as he also kept his position. Therefore, all of them were full members of the Secret Privy Council. Hence, the new Governor Mr Billsen should have been fairly certain that he could build his affairs and important secret and highly important matters of the Administration on this foundation.

However, when the Honourable Jurgen Billsen realised that he had been deceived, he eventually made his own announcement of the suspension of the members of the Privy Council. This followed immediately in the same year, at the start of October, before the peculiar, unheard of, unreasonable and unlawful, foolhardy rebellion and uprising at the Fortress Christiansborg. Mr Billsen now had reasons, as he put it, to realise their intrigues, then he felt so betrayed that he valued ever less their feigned sincerity.

Yet, returning to my own affairs and to continue properly for Your Excellency and the entire Honourable Gracious Gentlemen Directors, concerning blessed Governor Jurgen Billsen, the Company and the Fortress Christiansborg; the Governor's fatal and adventurous rule and the Administration as mentioned above, Mr Billsen finally, in the month of September decided to release them from their hitherto trusted and high ranking positions as members in the Secret Privy-Council and from their esteemed positions as councillors.

He suspended the entire Secret Privy-Council. In his explanation and procedure, he announced this publicly for all the Company's then functionaries, and thereby demonstrated what had been forced on him and that he had been prompted to send on the "journey" in writing, and should be read not only to the White functionaries in the service of the Company, but also to the entire military. This announcement took place on the large newly built bastion or battery whereas for the civilian functionaries it was announced at the hall of the Administration. Hopefully, this can be found in the Honourable Company's Offices amongst Mr Billsen's left behind documents that he kept during his time at Christiansborg Fortress.

[FREDERICUS DESCRIBES THE REBELLION AT CHRISTIANSBORG FORTRESS]

These people, embittered by Mr Billsen's new procedures and conditions, made many vile means and plots for revenge and dissatisfaction against Billsen, by suspending and removing him from the Administration, which also came to pass in the following way: by

The *Theologian* Slave Trader

creating a rebellion and uprising in the army against the Fortress and against Mr Billsen. They were pretending that it was due to Billsen's stinginess and particular interest in making deductions in their wages because most of them were in debt to the Company, or else they were charged more for the goods than the Company's prices allowed him to take and in this way he squeezed the blood out of all of them to his own benefit and advantage.

What happened then? One Sunday evening Monsieur Klein with the permission of the Governor, had been to the Dutch Fortress Creveceur, about 1,883 metres, just over a mile, away from Christiansborg Fortress, to visit the then Governor Balthazar Keyman. When he returned from there and after having held his domain and service, Monsieur Klein went down to the Master Builder and soldier Lochaus's room, to where he had previously had four bottles of distilled spirits brought down. This was made into punch, so that this alcoholic drink could be served to all army personnel. All of them were called, including the sentry who was also being relieved so he could take part in this gaiety. To make this gaiety all the more amusing, a fiddle had been provided and was played by Monsieur Abraham, the Fortress's Musician.

I could stand and watch this gaiety and much else as it was happening because my place was just opposite this room, though I had no light at that place where I was standing. When Monsieur Simon Klein argued on behalf of the Company, Mr Billsen disagreed with him with the following remarks:

"Can you imagine their finding and the circumstantial evidence, how some of them will say about you that you are "a sheep head" and incompetent in this position which was given you by Billsen".

"Had he not at all times performed his duties as a loyal and honest civil servant in the service of the Company?"

This the rebels proclaimed in unison amidst the refreshing punch and the delightful music.

"Now I am pleased", said Klein, and went over to his room. Right away he came back down again and he had another four bottles of distilled spirits with him. More punch was made, they sang and danced and he sang with these rebels from the Company.

They became more and more merry and were already singing louder and louder. Again Klein let yet another four bottles of spirits be brought over. According to rumours, all of the previously mentioned distilled spirits and that which was just brought in, had been obtained by Simon Klein from the suspended sergeant at arms, Cornelius Pedersen, for this occasion. It was not known, if this was by purchase or as a gift amongst friends.

This noise and commotion made Governor Billsen who was, it was said, getting ready to go to bed and had the vicar with him, quite amazed. Therefore, he sent for Messieurs Wilder and Platfod, both of whom were Head-Assistants, to go with full equipage to inquire why there was such a do at the Fortress and where it came from. When they found out what was happening, he sent these Messieurs to call Klein to come to him but Klein was deliberating whether he wanted to or did not want to. Then, at last he turned to his gathering and asked:

"Should I go or not to see the Governor?"

At this he hesitated a bit and then he quickly resolved with himself and said to his gathering and the soldiers:

"It does not matter, I will go."

Being drunk and crazy they all answered,

"Just go. We will see to the rest."

When he had come up to the Governor, Billsen asked Klein what had made him entertain in the soldiers' quarters at this peculiar time? Did he not know that it was improper for him, a former member of the Council? Did he not also know that once the tattoo had been struck, everything should be calm at the Fortress? Against this, Mr Klein objected and expressed his anger assuming that no one could forbid him to go wherever he wanted to go, be this in the soldiers' rooms, and there to be merry with them, as others had done this too.

While this was being ventilated with the Governor in the hall, all the

The *Theologian* Slave Trader

Fortress's military officers on the battery came in to the Governor's hall to find out what had happened to Simon Klein. Upon this, the Governor proclaimed that Klein should be taken to his own room as a prisoner. Klein protested very strongly against this arrest, slapped his hand on the table before the Governor and the Council, and was not willing to put up with the arrest. In spite of this, the Governor called for the Commanding Constable, Johan Ernst, and two men to put Klein into custody in his own room.

When the Constable arrived with his rifle commando to carry out the Governor's orders to command this quick operation, some or a couple of these crazy soldiers who were all armed, some with rifles, others with axes from the Fortress's stock and some with improvised weapons, there was nobody who would obey the orders from Governor Billsen. Just as before, they all said, with one united and agreeing voice and drunken mouths, that nobody should please obey the orders from this Commander. They were all protesting against Billsen's order, as well as against him as a person. They acknowledged and declared in public that they would not hereafter acknowledge him as their Governor and then, amongst other things, they began to cut into the walls and the staircase to the Governor's hall in the area around the battery, as well as in the staircase to the battery from the yard and to the room of Lechon, where these crazy, disturbed and conspiring soldiers had come from.

However, as all these people who were so embittered at the Governor, the honourable Mr Jurgen Billsen, were chopping and cutting everywhere around them, the Commanding Corporal arrived whom they might have chopped apart had he not quickly jumped to one side. All of this, which now and hereafter was and would be recorded, I confess to God with a clean conscience, has really happened in all its detail, as I went everywhere myself amongst these rebels, be it with the greatest officer, during this evening and throughout the night.

In this way, I could more carefully register all the occurring events in this situation and I was being affected, and was being reminded of my suffering. I also, was one who had suffered with all his heart, God be my witness, had sacrificed myself to serve honestly, upright and sincerely for the sake of the Lord, the Honourable Company here and, in whatever else I may be able to understand with the strength of my body and mind, the Governor my superior from the Board or the honourable Board itself, for any service either directly or indirectly according to my sworn duty and most humble obligation which I had always done before and which I uphold at this time. And after my very toilsome life in this world, under whatever circumstances and conditions, place and country in this world that God sees fit to lead and take me to in His wisdom's inscrutable counsel, forever until my last breath and death before a joyous resurrection and God's blessed countenance to see in the kingdom of the immortal peaceful kingdom, perpetually hold innocently, unchanging and entirely holy.

I shall now return to the previous content of my material from which I have deviated a little. During the previously mentioned tumult, it was declared in public by the entire army rank in the service of the Company at the Fortress Christiansborg, that Governor Billsen was a bloodhound, extortionist, swindler and much else which I shall refrain from mentioning in the presence of Your Excellency and all the Honourable and Gracious Gentlemen. Under this previously often mentioned great stir and noise, with embitterment and much anger and drunkenness, these miserable soldiers took over the authority of the Company as well as the authority of our common honourable Masters in order to take away, as well as remove, the responsible authority of Governor Billsen from the rule of the Administration at Christiansborg Fortress and, instead, install to their obvious preparation and purpose, a new Governor whom they assumed would rule and relate to them and pay their wages as they pleased, according to their will and at their discretion.

This unorganised election by this unorganised garrison and army at Christiansborg Fortress, after the dismissal of Billsen, and Klein's demands and claims on the battery for himself, first arrived at Simon Klein as a Governor who should, henceforth, govern as the Governor at the Fortress Christiansborg with subordinate Masters for lodgings and other affairs relevant as well as obligations: Ludvig Ferdinand Romer as Merchant and Joost Platfod as Bookkeeper, Secretary and Office Assistant.

The *Theologian* Slave Trader

Since Simon Klein, during all this noise and commotion on the battery with this merry making and during the formation of this newly established Administration, was the one on whom the responsibility of governorship had fallen, he went, in the meantime, into the hall to see Mr Billsen, who expostulated with him his committed big offence, which Mr Billsen judged as being the worst culprit's and traitor's serious misdeed to "Crimen Laesae Majestaetis".

By then, these mad soldiers were so impatient that they would not wait until Mr Billsen had spoken to Klein. Because of their dangerous shouting and screams, Billsen first had to please them by withdrawing his issued command, about which he was just powerless. He found his own person too frail to defend himself and, therefore, had to give in, after these people with the greatest impatience and bitterest anger, had chopped down both the walls and the staircase leading to the hall, in their anger and bitterness and now finally, also the door leading into the hall itself, where the Governor and the Council were gathered, in order to take Klein by force out from this Secret gathering. Because of their foolhardy attack and also out of fear of further extreme actions, Mr Billsen felt himself compelled and forced, not only to acquit Klein of the served arrest warrant, but even to release him after request from the rebels.

However, all this was not at all enough to please the disturbed soldiers. They continued to shout and scream still louder using much cursing and swearing which was only to be expected from such mad and drunken soldiers saying: "That bloodthirsty Billsen, he has sucked the blood from us; that rogue, that so and so, that evil so and so". Amidst those loud shouts and screams, they repeated once again their declaration of before: "Billsen, that bloodhound! This so and so! So and so on. Him as a Governor? No, we want a Governor who can and will give us our wages which we want in line with the Company's instructions according to the age and rank which this post could merit".

Because of the issues mentioned above, these disturbed people due to an irrevocable proof of their drunkenness and madness, happened to change their previous election of Simon Klein and then turned their minds and choice to Joost Platfod, a Head-Assistant. But Platfod, pretending to be inconvenienced by the ailments of old age and the nature of the conditions of the country, and coupled with the Administration's critical experience, publicly refused. Eventually they authorised Private Christen Lind to go and collect the keys from Mr Billsen to which Billsen objected, but with use of force and a 'Still-Holbyarm' (hand weapon) in his hand, Private Lind forcefully tore the keys out of Mr Billsen's hands and brought them to his comrades who were standing outside in the meantime to watch how the dismissed and suspended Governor Billsen would react to this. Had he not volunteered to give up in the end, they would have been able to use other means with which to obtain the keys against Billsen's will, according to the mood these foolish and rather pathetic and brainless people were in.

After the acquisition of the mentioned keys and following that Monsieur Platfod had refused this temporary, so to speak, vacant Administration, a new assembly on the battery was convened and all the people who attended agreed to call a new election, which was the joint decision of the people, who in the end, arrived at the approval of the previously announced Billsen's suspension from this Secret Privy Council at Christiansborg, and also as the Chief Merchant at the other Fortress, Fredensborg.

Then Simon Klein, who accepted this same election and Administration though on the previously made conditions of having one's affairs on reasonably safe ground for the future and, in addition, to have some authorized pretext at his disposal because this uprising at some point in the future, God willing, the Honourable Board might decide to investigate and, according to information, look into the true state of affairs and those found guilty in this case, in accordance with the just law in Denmark, eventually would be given the judgement that the court for such an important case would find to be right.

Simon Klein, a person with some brains in his head, could probably see that in the future, this uprising, God willing, would be looked at more closely, then he would discreetly like to have this uprising on his side in such a way that, in this event, nothing should prejudice

The *Theologian* Slave Trader

him. Thus, he and other civilian functionaries took me, Fredericus as their witness on this, before he took up this vacant Administration which Jurgen Billsen now on this occasion, and this far, was suspended from. However, upon this, he received the same status, no differently, until the arrival of the first ship from Copenhagen.

Monsieur Ludvig Ferdinand Romer, who at the beginning of the aforementioned uprising, had lain down to rest some time previously in bed in the usual quarter for him on the battery underneath Mr Billsen's above mentioned hall, and from this place Romer could hear what was happening and he could hear just as well the uproar coming from the battery from the soldiers' new change to the Administration at the Fortress, claimed that he was fast asleep. As it happened, at the same time, these merry people and soldiers "killed two birds with one stone", as you say in common language, because as soon as they dismissed the appointed Governor who was dispatched to them by the Board, they also used their self-assumed and great authority in this field to dismiss the two Messieurs, Billsen, and Romer. Then they appointed two Head-Assistants to the Secret Privy-Council, namely Messieurs Thomas Broch and Johan Wilder.

Of those two Messieurs, the first who was Thomas Broch was not at this time or during this evening here at the Fortress Christiansborg at the unexpectedly occurring uproar and rebellion, but was at Ningo's Fredensborg Fortress and at his post as trusted Merchant. However, some days later, he finally arrived at Christiansborg Fortress after orders from the new Governor Klein and the new Council in order that he and a colleague, though now also dismissed in relation to Billsen and who did not therefore have great credit in the Secret Privy-Council along with other civilian staff, were summoned to be witnesses. They were going to give their testimony concerning what took place at Christiansborg Fortress during those days with regard to Simon Klein's strange, notable yet very short rule as "President", according to the then decision to have him as the " Governor 'ad Interim Extraordinairus" to be able to deal with the foreigners at other European Fortresses.

[FREDERICUS WRITES ABOUT THE SHORT GOVERNORSHIP: "AD INTERIM EXTRAORDINAIRUS" OF SIMON KLEiN]

The achievement of his short rule had the following content of which a little will here be demonstrated. Signeur Simon Henriksen Klein became the Governor "ad interim extraordinairus", or the interim President ruler at the Fortress Christiansborg, according to the final, decision. A title which may please the foreign European nations' representatives or Governors, on the coast, for example, The English or The Dutch representatives or Governors. In order to fulfil in all possible manners and in the most humble way the precise content of Your Excellency's most gracious order, I here in my humble fulfilment and most dutiful and obliging account, which includes even the smallest circumstances for the sake of necessary clarity and easy understanding, I have observed and passed on with the greatest diligence. For this reason and purpose, I will start with this unusual Administration and rule, by describing it with what is most convenient regarding the previous positions, namely Governor, "ad Interim Extraordinairus", and so on.

Throughout the entire night, the appointed Governor Simon Henriksen Klein was in his usual room with Monsieur Ludvig Ferdinand Romer at the Fortress where they had an open banquet for the soldiers throughout the entire night, owing to the perpetual people who wished to negotiate and, therefore, people kept flocking there, including people from this new Administration as well as people connected to the Secret Privy-Council at the Fortress.

This happened with such pleasure, that it could well look as if this had been arranged with advance applied diligence and a merriment during which this newly appointed Governor appeared very pleased and happy although I, sometimes, when I had the honour of seeing and talking with him, had to acknowledge, with his wise face and his soft heart, that he could not possibly be able to foresee and learn from experience and daily experience that remarkably and importantly, could bring upon any significance and considerable difficulty, as well as bring far-reaching consequences and mishaps along. This situation could not possibly have any successful end when this, at some point, it would be judged at a suitable place, and this would be done in such a manner that people with some kind of honour and reputation could not recover. So it also happened here with our new ruler at Christiansborg Fortress.

However for Ludvig Ferdinand Romer it was very different as he turned out to be a man of much greater courage and boldness as well as wisdom about the correctness of the case where the same was of such great diffuseness. He assured these unsteady people of great things, namely, that now, they would, henceforth, receive what the Company granted them, such as gold as their wages or goods after the price of gold. In addition, they could only safely rely on what the Governor, Billsen, had previously defrauded them and deducted from their wages to seek his own unlawful gain and profit. This should be restored to them and upon this everybody, indeed all of us, were and became absolutely delighted.

In order that everything could have the appearance of orderliness and prudence, Klein and Romer, on the following day, sent for the Governors or Merchants of the foreign English and Dutch Fortresses to come and express their points of view so that nothing in the future should turn out to their disadvantage. These people did also occasionally appear in order to bring about peace and calm at our Danish Fortress Christiansborg, but it was all in vain. The obdurate soldiers were standing more than was fair on the side of Simon Klein, although Mr Billsen opposed strongly to this. But the strangers did resolve that Billsen should maintain his present rank and seat as previously, when he was ruling the Administration, even though Simon Henrik Klein should act as, and be titled as, the future Colony Manager and President "Ad Interim". Thus and in this way, Klein should administrate the rule of the Administration of the Fortress Christiansborg on 9 out of 10 days.

Still, what cleverness could Billsen employ in the meantime? Billsen was a person who was very determined both in terms of getting ideas as well as making use of good advice; an individual who, in time, seemed to have great plans for the Administration, therefore was anxious to see to it that activities for this honourable Company were not neglected at this time either, as everything pointed towards a good settlement and a calm disposition again. All seemed to aim for a good restitution and improvement on the previous situation. For this purpose, he first equipped himself with the necessary, previous clever advice from the past, namely, he let the two Messieurs Simon Klein and Ludvig Ferdinand Romer be sent for in discretion, for them to meet in privacy so that they could be reconciled amongst themselves so that Klein and Romer could have their posts back and what ever else could be settled through negotiation, either by the Board in Copenhagen or through another proper process. Billsen then promised to please the soldiers hereafter with an advance on their wages, alternately, in 'Bosh' and then, alternately, in goods.

However, these people did not let themselves be appeased with these reasonable promises and conditions. Then Klein turned round and now changed his mind saying; "Here you have the keys. Now you can turn whoever you like into a Governor". Upon this and thereafter, Billsen continued in the Administration. The further development on this case can be found in "Acta Procesus" (official company reports), beginning in December in the year of 1744 and continued until the death of Billsen. The death certificate was signed by myself and Surgeon Carl Engman, thus authorized at the beginning of the process by the then Governor Billsen with the following orders in the document; "XXX, Sub. Litr. D", which was sent home to the Board in Copenhagen with the ship named "Williamina Galley", which departed from the coast in the year of 1746 under the command of Captain Boyesen.

As regards my own affairs during the times of this great man Billsen, he was at first quite courteous and polite towards me. When he heard about my circumstances during Jurgensen's term, he became somewhat amazed. Thus, during his time, an order was issued from the Board that I had been permitted to return to Denmark, but he thought that with my bad circumstances it would not be advisable to do so, by going back early on the ship on which he arrived himself, the "Williamina Galley". Therefore, he persuaded me to wait for another opportunity to leave the Coast on board a different ship as perhaps, by then my situation would be more favourable if God would give His blessing.

It is true, that I heard from somebody and I also learned this myself from Billsen who said that those who had anything owed to them in their wages, could have goods, in particular the Parish Clerk. Yet, I have to acknowledge on this given occasion, that afterwards when these well-made promises should be put into action, I sensed that Mr Billsen was a human being who was equally subject to the same condition as all children of 'Adam', namely fickleness. As when I wanted to have two pieces of 'callevapper' on my wages I could not have any but was offered other goods which could not be traded without any damage. Eventually, I got goods for or on my outstanding wages under the price that he then saw fit to charge, yet I had to pay more for them than I had done some time previously under his predecessor.

[FREDERICUS WRITES ABOUT GOVERNOR BILLSEN'S DEATH]

The circumstances surrounding Mr Jurgen Billsen's death were as follows. When the above- mentioned affair was at its strongest development, he unexpectedly had an attack but nobody knew by what illness. Within a few days he became weak and as he had only a little faith in the chances of being cured by our surgeon because he was a foreigner from Sweden, therefore he sent for the Dutch surgeon to treat him. This surgeon attended him for a couple of days without success. But strangely, the last time, in the evening, in his drunkenness, this surgeon gave out the following words to some Negroes in the Negro hamlet:

"Now, I have administered something to Billsen and if he lives until tomorrow, then Billsen has a strong constitution, as it is impossible, considering his circumstances and the nature and strength of the administered strong medicine, that he can live on".

The Danish barber, Engman, also heard this from the surgeon who also said, somewhat suspiciously, that Billsen would not live until the next morning, but he did live until the evening of the following day. This "Butcher" had contact with the local wife of the arrested Corporal Cornelius Petersen, who was sent to prison by Billsen. This surgeon was entertaining and enjoying various favours from this Corporal's local wife, called Anne Sophie. In the meantime, Anne Sophie was the daughter of the local Medicineman, who was known in the whole area to be notoriously wicked, and had therefore, bewitched Governor Billsen and all of his sympathizers and doing so at great cost, for letting Corporal Cornelius Petersen, his son-in-law, remain in prison.

But prior to his rapid death, after he had taken communion from me, Billsen informed me though only with expressions and gestures, that I who was well informed would have to be constant in this and that, concerning his left and still developing case, I would allow right and justice and not let anybody influence me neither now nor in the future.

About this I have here most humbly given Your Excellency my recollection of the following content. Mr. Billsen died in my arms and on the following day was buried with the usual ceremony after he had been ruling from the 2nd of February 1744 until the middle of March in the year 1745.

[FREDERICUS WRITES ABOUT GOVERNORS PLATFOD AND BROCH]

Following Now The Accession Of Thomas Broch
To The Administration, His Management Of The Administration
And His Peculiar Death, Etc.

Following the death of Governor Billsen, the Governorship was offered to Joost Platfod, who ceded this due to lack of authority and in accordance with rank and order. The successor was Thomas Broch, former Merchant at Fredensborg Fortress. He was sober and sensible, courteous and respectable; an individual who could have been very useful on the Coast. People had been hoping that, over time he could have done a beneficial service to the Company if God had granted and endowed him with a longer life. How regrettable! His life was only very short before it was cut off from the Administration, almost before he became a Governor. He had not even assessed the affairs of his predecessor with necessary diligence as is suitable, but mere assessment of the warehouses from the outside and very roughly so, in the presence of me and some civilian staff, as well as the Company's gold chest which was found to be rather light.

The *Theologian* Slave Trader

The circumstances surrounding his death were the following: ten days after his election and accession to the Administration, he hosted his first traditional entertainment, as Governor, for everybody, Blacks as well as Whites. For the Blacks in one way with tobacco, distilled spirits and then "panchises", a kind of gift, which were given to the most senior members of the Council, the Administration and the Council of the Negro hamlet.

When the foreign guests and the Governor Merchants and Managers from their Fortresses, Mr. Dithmar from the English Fortress and Mr Balthazar Koymans from the Dutch Fortress, had left with their subordinates, the Dutch Governor as he was called, namely Koymans, invited Broch over for dinner on the second day. He excused himself, just for fun, and promised nevertheless that he would keep the appointment if he did not have any unavoidable cause for absence or be seized by any ugly illness, which unfortunately did happen. That same evening, when we the civilian staff members were sitting at dinner with the Governor, Governor Mr Broch said that one should not wish for anything. He said this in jest and that yet he might well wish for a small refreshing fever so that tomorrow he would have an adequate reason and excuse for not going. He was shrinking away from being the object of circumstantial discussions at this early stage of his Governorship, and I, if I should say this myself, was a particularly good friend of his and the vicar, Mr Peter Meyer, and I was keeping him company constantly during this difficult early start to his rule, by resting with him in the hall.

However, very early in the morning after the Saturday's hosting, when he woke up and then I woke up myself, as I was lying in the bed with him, and then I also went to keep him company for a small stroll on the battery in order to get some fresh air as he thought he had an ear problem, I comforted him as best as I could, saying that this might just be a small cold that would soon pass. At 6 o'clock the same morning, I had to leave him to go to church to seek to perform my duties. When I finished performing my duties, and having requested permission to see him, I went up to him again, and hour by hour he became worse and worse with incredible pains in his stomach and around the bellybutton which made him very anxious. I had to stay with him all the time as he wanted to talk about heavenly matters.

He could feel death and he died on the night before the Tuesday in the same strange manner that also ended the lives of many other people at the same time at the Fortress. In his case, he was only lying in bed for a few hours so that it did not look like any serious illness as compared to the other cases, so that he did not give up in even the smallest way, as only in the area around the bellybutton where he was troubled by such an extreme pain and unspeakable suffering according to his own uttering. Over the night this pain spread further and further into other parts and limbs of his body and eventually they gathered in a great many knots at the heart and, under much real obvious pain, his chest moved up and down to the heart, with much agony and pain around it, he finally collapsed and made one last movement and stopped. This released the most pitiful sympathies from all the compassionate onlookers and those staying with him.

When people suffered this kind of fast attack, some had 2 to 3 days of their lives left and some 5 to 6 days at most. In such instances they were troubled as they were bedridden without more than a moment between pains that could be so powerful that they would think they were drawing their last breath. Although after the first attack a person might not give up the ghost right away, but in this same way many people would die and, with the same painful fear and torment, a person would have to leave the world upon God's chosen time and hour, in this manner and at this time like the Governor. All the many people who would die hereafter at this time and place, namely Christiansborg Fortress, did in the beginning, have the same conditions in the same way, with the very same circumstances so that all of them, after they died, were pale on the cheeks which was common with dead people, as well as blue on the lips and underneath the eyes, on the nails, behind the ears, the toes and so on; occasionally with foam and considerable froth coming from their mouths.

These were unusual accidents with so many dead people at a point when we were not that many people at the Fortress Christiansborg and yet, out of the people who were here, some died needlessly so that we could hardly bury them as soon as they died as, when we some times were in the process of burying people and had hardly

The *Theologian* Slave Trader

placed them properly in the ground, then others, who had been lying there twitching in the meantime, also died.

These happenings, involving many dead people at this peculiar time, were said by rumours over the entire land, to be due to genuine poisoning which the Negroes did believe to be true and that such conditions existed and could be proved. This, it was believed, could have been brought into the Fortress Christiansborg on behalf of the former Sergeant at Arms, Cornelius Petersen, due to his case and for his sake in order to obtain his release from prison.

According to common rumours and reports amongst everybody, including even the children, the poison had been brought in to be used at the Fortress in order to exterminate, in the first instance, the Administration and the sympathizers of Mr Billsen and indeed the entire Honourable Danish Business Community, until the most lowly soldier could and should come to take his place in the Administration and then also that Cornelius Petersen, in the same instance, could come out to freedom, and again to be much more reasonable, to come to work in the Administration itself.

Such an un-heard of misdeed, it was suggested, had been devised by Cornelius Petersen and his accomplice. Devised in order to disrupt and destroy the Fortress Christiansborg, all the affairs of the legal Danish Business Community on the Coast of Guinea in Africa, to bring an irreparable disadvantage and harm to the Honourable Company.

In this way, my very highly respected friend, now blessed with the lord, left so to speak, the world and his recently assumed Administration all too early. A man who was so dearly loved by both Blacks and Whites, very honoured and held in high esteem, sober and good-natured, respectable and decent, sensible, wise and very thoughtful in all his beginning affairs. Indeed, to put it shortly, Governor Thomas Broch was an individual who was expected to do much good over time. He died after having only worked in the service of the Company for 12 days as Governor; most regrettable and pitiful.

Christiana Knudsen

[FREDERICUS WRITES ABOUT GOVERNOR JOHANNES WILDERS]

Honourable Johannes Wilders' Succession
And Assumption Of The Rule And The
Administration And The Short Time Of Rule.

As Joost Platfod now as previously had excused himself, Johannes Wilder took over this vacant Governorship. He was an individual about whom one could not see anything wise for the use and benefit of the Company. He was entirely without experience in the affairs of the Coast, he had only moderate intelligence and he was given to drink and women. He kept a Negro woman. The Administration to which he was properly elected, he had accepted according to custom. It was offered to him as the highest ranking person in the Secret Privy-Council and as people could not persuade Monsieur Platfod to take up the post due to his own excuses and by his self-acknowledged inexperience which he professed now as well as previously to the entire group of the civil members of the Secret Privy-Council. Therefore, they were obliged, according to instructions of the regular administration of the Company's affairs, or required to have a person with a certain experience of the Administration, which simply had to be a person from the Secret Privy-Council, of whom all were civilians. In addition, at this point in time with shortages of people, the Secret Privy-Council, in a fully orderly and customary fashion, were unavoidably compelled and forced to elect this person for the Administration.

During the beginning of his rule, Governor Wilders conducted himself orderly and very carefully, and was determined to conclude Mr Billsen's case and ongoing process, in order to bring this to finiteness, which did not happen but remained at the end in the same state in which Mr Billsen had left it. This was so as his days and life in the Administration were short. He died in the same manner and under the same circumstances as his predecessor, Thomas Broch. The rumour that this death as well as the former and the following deaths were carried out by means of a poison, became stronger with this death. It became more obvious and evident to have happened for the sake of the afore-mentioned arrested Cornelius Petersen and to have been caused by his wife. Thus, Mr Johannes Wilder left the Administration and died in late April in the year of 1745, after he had managed this for one month.

[FREDERICUS WRITES ABOUT GOVERNOR AUGUST HACHENBERG]

August Friderich Hachenberg, His Election And Assumption To The Governorship, Rule And Final Replacement.

Since Monsieur Platfod was now the only member of the Secret Privy-Council remaining, and who had on some occasions previously refused the election to the Administration, he also now on this occasion after Christiansborg Fortress's then unhappy and moral chaotic events, refused the offer and therefore the order went back to Hachenberg who recently had been promoted under Wilder from Under Assistant to Head Assistant in the Secret Privy-Council and Merchant for Fredensborg Fortress. By God's assistance and supplication of the civilian ranks in the church and the vicar Reverend Mr Peder Meyer at a ceremony grading for an "Ad Interim" installation, Hachenberg became the next Governor. He was a young person with good natural gifts; an individual who followed the necessary conduit for the received and accepted Administration as well as the use and advantage of such a position and he was also industrious.

At the assumption of the Governorship, he inspected the Company's warehouses, as had his predecessors, while he was in the Secret Affairs dealing with those matters relating to the honourable Company. He kept secret, as did his two predecessors, as to with what rights and loyalty this was administrated, therefore, these matters were unbeknown to some of us. If anybody were to have knowledge of this, it would have been Governor Joost Platfod, who at that time was the only remaining member of the Secret Privy-Council on the Guinea Coast.

According to common rumours, Hachenberg acted rather suspiciously, such as, in the year of 1746, a few days before the arrival of the "Williamina Galley" to the waters of Christiansborg Fortress, which at that time was lying at Cap d'Corso Fortress, the main English Fortress, some miles west of Christiansborg Fortress from where Monsieur Ludvig Ferdinand Romer had boarded this ship coming from Copenhagen, he wrote a letter, which was supposed to be coming from Copenhagen for Monsieur Joost Platfod. This letter contained a congratulation message starting thus:

"According to the will of the Lawful Board to the Honourable Monsieur Platfod for the Governorship at Christiansborg ...."

This tricky letter was supposed to be coming from Copenhagen, stating that Platfod was the newly appointed Head Merchant at Christiansborg Fortress, and that Simon Henriksen Klein was the Merchant at the Fortress Fredensborg at Ningo. This false news eventually reached Mr August Friderich Hachenberg, the "Ad Interim" Governor, and affected him somewhat seriously, and therefore, he certainly seemed to take care and to spend time ensuring that his own affairs would be in order before the hand over. His ingenuity and accuracy showed, in that he stole many things. He, on a Sunday, let bring out of the Company's warehouse, a considerable amount of gunpowder and flintlocks, more than 3 men's head loads, to be brought to the Governor of the Dutch Fortress, besides a large part which he let stay with Monsieur Negotiator Aclovi, as people called him, who was Hachenberg's father-in-law, under the pretext that he was negotiating these goods for his son-in-law.

However, the goods that were transported to the Dutch Governor were in order to clear a bill between him and the Dutch Governor, although 8 days previously Hachenberg had himself confessed in the presence of many people, especially me and the barber Engman, that he did not owe him anything.

In addition, on the same Sunday afternoon, he let 30 or 40 slaves of different gender and size be transported, some to the Dutch Fortress and the remaining to the English Fortress on the pretext that, that too was due to debt. This action was just as strange and it was suspicious.

The *Theologian* Slave Trader

A peculiar debt about which nobody knew, neither could anybody find out anything about this, and nobody even could understand it, since, according to his own confession it was not for any known Company debt which had been amassed during the term of Christen Glob Dorph. Moreover, how Hachenberg had related to the above and on what basis this had in fact taken place, nobody knew other than presumably Mr Platfod, who was with him at that same time during the entire afternoon.

At first he, Platfod, walked with him, Hachenberg to the Dutch Fortress and then, later on, to the English Fortress, giving the reason that he wanted to complete all preparations, but as to the importance of these visits, I present this matter for the most gracious attention of Your Excellency and the Honourable Board.

With regard to the case which was begun by Mr Billsen, the Governor, Hachenberg did not wish to concern himself with it to begin with, therefore, conditions under which he let myself and surgeon Carl Engman sign this document of this case were terrible as we were the only survivors with knowledge of the case and, in addition, we had been acting as observers on the case. Still, he occupied himself much with this case later and gave his reason that there was a lack of staff at the Fortress because of the powerful and daily rampant deaths at the Fortress Christiansborg,

Hachenberg then worked out a means by which he could release two old soldiers, Christian Lochan and Blocher, who were put in irons when arrested by order of Mr Billsen at Elmina, the main Dutch Fortress, pending further development in the case. Though, some time before, during the development of this case, they had been taken from there and brought to Christiansborg Fortress. He allowed them to be released and made them swear the usual oath of allegiance.

From the Company's service, Cornelius Petersen together with the other Assistants who had long been put into prison at the Fortress Christiansborg, now gained their freedom from prison. Hachenberg was driven to this decision by the common rumour that before a certain time he would surely die if Cornelius Petersen did not gain his freedom as, because of Petersen's imprisonment, two previous Governors had died by use of certain means. In addition, an express messenger arrived, namely Anniche from Merchant Mr Dithmar at the English Fortress, who through the English Commission warned that, in order to save the young life of Hachenberg, he must have a serious conversation with Cornelius Petersen and let him lose in case he, Hachenberg did not want to lose his life within 14 days, which not only I, but indeed many others had heard, too.

At length, Hachenberg was, on the arrival of the "Williamina Galley", replaced by former Head Assistant and Council member Joost Platfod who was conferred by the Administration. At that point, Hachenberg had managed the Administration as "Ad Interim" from the beginning of May in the year of 1745 until the 17th of June 1746.

[FREDERICUS WRITES ABOUT JOOST PLATFOD'S GOVERNORSHIP]

Honourable Joost Platfod
Governor And Colony Manager
At The Fortress Christiansborg
His Assumed Rule And Governorship, Etc.

The previous Governor, "Ad Interim" Mr August Friderich Hachenberg was replaced by Monsieur Joost Platfod, previous Head Assistant and 2nd vote in the Secret Privy-Council who was sent to the Coast by the honourable Company on the 2nd of February in the year 1744, together with the stationed Governor Mr Jurgen Billsen, now blessedly departed, as Head Assistant in the Secret Privy-Council. As Platfod had a certain age, the Board could probably have expected considerable services by him on the Coast of Guinea but, regrettably, his certain experience had been contradicted at Christiansborg Fortress. He, in his time as Head Assistant and vote in the Secret Privy-Council, had offered less services than was expected, given his mature age and considerable rank at Christiansborg Fortress, he was less attentive towards the Company or to any staff in his entire time as Head Assistant, and less hereafter, as far as was known to me during my time on the Coast.

The *Theologian* Slave Trader

Monsieur Joost Platfod, in his rank as Head Assistant and in the Council during the time of Mr Billsen, as well as other times, conducted himself in such a manner that everybody who was impartial and with a fair mind must acknowledge and testify with a clear conscience that he was and had been an individual without so much drive. He also lacked initiative for the service of the Honourable Company that he, with his own honest and sincere confession, often publicly confessed and declared. The indecisive manner in which he conducted himself as head Assistant in the Secret Privy-Council at the time of the known and widely rumoured rebellion amongst the army, and other interested parties at Christiansborg Fortress, against Mr Billsen became obvious through Monsieur Platfod's softness in nature and inexperience considering his mature age and considerable rank.

Under these dangerous circumstances, during the rebellion at Christiansborg Fortress, the Governor, Mr Billsen, was absolutely forced to apply lawful procedures against, not only Monsieur Joost Platfod, but even, in particular, with respects to these two Messieurs Simon H. Klein and Ludvig Ferdinand Romer, whose stance and behaviour in all fairness could be called and described as the driving forces and supporters in this very dangerous and harmful rebellion against the Governor and the welfare of the entire Company on the Coast of Guinea.

While this came to pass at Christiansborg Fortress, Mr Billsen conceived, and probably not without reason, strong concerns about Monsieur Platfod, who seemed to be interested in these two Messieurs, Klein and Romer, who, he presumed, were the driving negative forces in those difficult decline times at Christiansborg Fortress. Billsen, therefore became not only reserved towards Platfod the longer this went on, but also avoided having any close contact with him even as a member of the Secret Privy-Council and soon avoided any direct current and future dealings with him in the same way as he was reserved towards the two above-mentioned and partial parties in this case, namely Klein and Romer.

This registered with Monsieur Platfod and every day he could sense the Governor's ever increasing resentment towards his person and this could well have resulted in more severe and further actions. But

Monsieur Platfod, along with many others, was also not unaware about how much favour I enjoyed from Governor Billsen, although the Governor knew also that I was friendly towards Platfod and the other two Messieurs, namely Klein and Romer.

Platfod was once complaining and opened his heart to me and announced that he was suspected of knowing about the rebellion and asked, therefore, if I would make an effort to make Mr Billsen more friendly towards him. This, I was ready and willing to do and I did and I managed to bring about this effect in the Governor who, thereafter, treated Platfod with more respect though not as a Council member but as a respected Head Assistant. I went to this great length for Mr Platfod but in what way did this man reward me for my well deserved efforts?

There were untruthful and less respectful rumours about me coming from Mr Platfod, and indeed, most likely from the Honourable Board, too. So my gracious gentlemen could themselves offer a regrettable proof of this deceitful gratitude towards me and this unfair discrimination against me which had always been my usual fortune and reward at Christiansborg Fortress; persecution, shame and harm, injustice and ungratefulness had hitherto been my well deserved thanks for my merits.

God is my true witness, and the cleanliness of my conscience. I speak the truth before God, I do not lie, and this was my greatest reward. As to what else concerning Platfod's capacity and competence as Head Assistant on the Guinea Coast, I hope will be established most graciously in the following information, as it was not only his sympathy for the rebellion that annoyed Mr Billsen, but also once when Platfod was offered the Governorship, he did, in fact, declare himself utterly unsuited for this exciting post due to his lack of experience with trade and management of the Administration.

Monsieur Platfod now accepted the Governorship, but at the previous election for this post, he was tacitly passed over and then they properly elected Monsieur Hachenberg instead. As mentioned, Monsieur Hachenberg was a young person who was quite passable and, I have to freely acknowledge, he cannot deny this himself, that due to my friendly and approachable company, conversation and unerring advice, which, for the sake of the Lord, although he subsequently, and according to the will of the High and Honourable Gentlemen Directors' gracious orders, had to resign and give way to Monsieur Platfod.

Yet, what use and advantage might the Company, in fact, had or expect from this ruling Governor I cannot say or write much about other than this, with a clear conscience, I can write about him that he was and was set to become a Governor, in the same vein as he was previously Head Assistant in the Secret Privy-Council. But how the Secret Privy-Council and the Administration at this time as well as previously have treated me with hate and persecution for my truthful witness in the Billsen case besides Romer's ugly abuse of pretending to be asleep during the rebellion, and I had to give evidence about this, has most humbly been reported to you in a journal for Your Excellency.

Monsieur Platfod has proved clearly to the entire world that he, by God's grace and great providence, has himself fallen into the grave that he wished to throw me into, namely, that it came to my knowledge, through the ship which had recently arrived on the Guinea Coast, that Mr Platfod, this old man, had taken pleasure in accompanying a young Mulatto-woman, that was hitherto believed to be his niece, Helena Svendsdatter. Praise to God, my benefactor, who always grants me victory and triumph over my enemies through Jesus Christ. Amen. Hallelujah!

Although Romer is a competent person in the service of the Company, and as he wished to advance in the world, it was soon rumoured that he was holding a reserved post, which had since been arranged by the Assistant Winkelmann, at the Company's Trading Post at Ada for him to trade. However, the same too had once been arranged for Hachenberg supposedly, but now he was personally occupied with other important affairs and he was not a mean person. If I may put it this way, he had certain ambition and, after his former cast off Negro woman, he had taken in a Mulatto-woman, perhaps in order to satisfy himself, after the famous English Proverb, "Varietas Delectat". He had been searching for refreshment in his pleasure at this change in line with the agreed tradition and custom of the country and the Fortress.

Monsieur Simon Klein in this new Administration let myself and surgeon Carl Engman express a protest concerning Mr Billsen's affairs that was ignored, but followed in "Vidimer et Copie Sub. Litr. F" (the Company's official report). Upon this, followed the declaration, "Sub. Ltr. G", from this Administration. I did not have much more to refer to since I, approximately one month later, received my dismissal about which here follows: "Sub. Ltr. H". In addition, I had obtained from the vicar, Reverend Peter Meyer, the requested Testimonial, that concerns my conduct and affairs that were also referred to in the "Sub. Litr. J" (the Company's official report). These, most humbly, I submit to you and I have nothing further to write about this good man Mr Joost Platfod than what is most necessary, that he was better suited as a good and honest conventional man in Copenhagen than Governor on the Coast of Guinea in Africa.

[FREDERICUS CONCLUDES]

MY MOST HUMBLE AND MODEST THOUGHTS CONCERNING THE
COAST OF GUINEA
IN AFRICA: ITS USEFUL AND MOST NECESSARY REFORMATION AND
IMPROVEMENT IN THE FUTURE TO THE USE AND ADVANTAGE
OF THE HONOURABLE COMPANY AND ALL ITS
SUBORDINATE STAFF IN THE HONOUR
OF GOD AND THEIR COMMON
BENEFIT IN THE NAME OF
JESUS CHRIST. AMEN!

By God's great mercy Your Excellency has granted me your special ray of grace that has rested on me, your most humble servant. With many years of inexperience and a short life of humblest discretion, I must confess to God with a clear conscience that, for this reason, Your Excellency by God's mercy, has been better towards me than ten fathers. Your particular mercy towards me, I will for as long as I have a breath of life inside me, carry as a living mark in the most humble and special gratitude stamped in my heart by God's fingers until my death and beyond.

The *Theologian* Slave Trader

When I, hereafter in my days of exile, have fought the good fight of fate and have commanded my spirit into the hands of God, a blessed departing in peace from this troubled and toilsome world, from these "Kedan's Pauluner", to peace before God, the calm and rest of the Sabbath which is best for God's people, landing in the port of calm in the Heaven in the joyous rooms in God's house and in Jerusalem over time, then the tears shall be wiped from the eyes and God's own true, eternal, independent really genuine joy and complacent pleasure shall delight the hearts of all faithful. Indeed, they shall join the song of the "Lamb" (in the Christian Bible) and so forth. Your Excellency, I going through my ordeal, has demonstrated to me your great mercy and your good deeds towards me.

As an obvious proof of this your great mercy and gracious kind heartedness towards me, Your Excellency has shown particularly a remarkable sign of mercy by this, your graciously issued order to me to put my humble Explanation and Declaration in writing, which has been written down and processed in this modest work. And, in so far as I am a mortal human being, I could not possibly exist in this frailty, having attempted, by God's mercy, to fulfil my most humble duty and obligation in order to observe most carefully the compliance and correction of this order reminding me of my obligation and duty. Now finally and in the end, I have observed and treated finally to the end, Your Excellency's gracious order, and this will, also, in accordance with my modest judgement and ten years of experience on the Coast in the service of the honourable Company as a Parish Clerk and Catechist, indeed fulfil in God's honour only your order demanding my sworn duty to the Company regarding my explanation, which I have thus fulfilled most humbly.

According to my simple thoughts and incomplete mind and experience, in relation to the state of affairs on the Coast, I expect, by God's assistance and blessing and therefore hope, for a future of improved situation from henceforth, which I have already been writing about in a more lengthy manner than I had anticipated at the start of this work in hand. And then, it is necessary that my thoughts turn, first of all, to the reformation of the rule of the Administration in the future. This could be administered in a better and more advantageous manner than at the present time, for the sake of the Honourable Company and all there, presumably at present as working staff, so that the most high ranking command, a "Governor", could be changed a little and favoured with such a title as "Director General", like the title of similar office in the Dutch nation. That is how the highest ranking Commander at the main Fortress Dutch Elmina is known.

Some years ago, this Dutch nation had, to the affront of our nation, established and organised their affairs in such a manner that the previously called Merchants at this Fortress situated near us and at several other Fortresses located up and down the coast, were hence forth, called Governors in order to make them equal to our Governors at Christiansborg Fortress. This has led to several complicated incidences that indeed, have been to the disadvantage and harm of Danish affairs.

Next, the lawful and legal Administration of the law should be strictly enforced, if the Board so please, for the sake of maintaining their own high authority and as well in order to administrate and enforce predominance and authority against all embezzlement in the trade amongst high and low staff members of all ranks so as to prevent, hinder and control in future, such cheating, so that the advantage to the Company will be the only and most important purpose and focus in all their work. This then becomes the only thing that everyone ever has to focus on, to believe in and to honestly and faithfully serve. The staff members should be well suitable and qualified, each in accordance to his rank and station. All possible defects and shortcoming in everything which could be of use and advantage at any time, be this night or day, should be vigilantly watched, for fraud and craftiness, not merely at happenings in the past, but just as much to repair these happenings now so that everything happens for the best in the future with the help of God, that searches and spread and transmits.

Then the King and the Kingdom of Denmark and Norway with their subordinate masters' honour and reputation and the increase of the flourishing and wealth and finally that of the Company as the nearest predominant authority for the Danish affairs on the Coast of Guinea in Africa, their constantly great use and advantage, needs to be attended to and promoted, so that the harm and damage to the Honourable Company is hindered and prevented. Then, at the end, the timely and constant welfare of each member of staff is attempted and carefully taken into consideration, all of this in the end, that everything must happen in God's honour, for the reputation of the King and the Administration and for the welfare and progress of the Honourable West Indian and Guinea Company.

All of this to observe, and to observe with vigilance, the necessity of all my humble thoughts require, that the Honourable Board will see fit to send a suitable individual, who holds dear God in his soul and conscience and his honour and reputation. Such person ought to be nominated as General Fiscal of the entire Coast of Guinea in Africa. A position of such a high authority in rank, action and seat ought not only be equal to a Director General but, even if it so pleases, be above it, concerning the Company's use, in order to seek and promote the administration of the law.

Moreover, in addition, more Fortresses and Lodgings should be established on the Coast. The authority of the Administration and the Council should be made each with a stable and equal basis. The entrusted staff of the power of each authority ought, with particular grace and honour and character, to report and adorn the honour and reputation of the Honourable Board itself whose eminent staff, such as Managing Clerks and others of authority, present and produce, for example, the General Fiscal of the entire Coast etc. in addition to the aforementioned "Director General" to be the most eminent thereafter.

The authority of the Administration and the Council should be organized based on each their own clear, stable and equal but separate duties. The entrusted staff of the power of each authority ought, with particular grace and honour and character, to report, as well as adore and show honour, to the reputation of the Honourable Board itself. The Board's eminent staff, such as Managing Clerks and other authorities, should also produce and present for example, the General Fiscal of the Company's entire trading activities etc. on the

Coast, and that the aforementioned "Director General's" office should be considered the most eminent there on the Danish Guinea Coast.

Thereafter, everybody, in descending order from this Authority's positions, who is connected to the Secret Privy-Council, will take part in an election, as it is also necessary to nominate an Executive for the Fortress Fredensborg, a Head Merchant at the Fortress Christiansborg and, in addition, a General Bookkeeper Merchant. When these necessities have been carried out, ordinary Head-Assistants in the Secret Privy-Council and for the Court's Administration, the General Fiscal person should oversee that everything will take place in an orderly, Christian and lawful manner. Then if he, so graciously believes and so pleases, he should have an adjutant in the form of a Fiscal Officer who could be sent out to watch and inspect, if possible, in all the various activities in the different departments.

These people, including each and every functionary in the service of the most lawful Company, from the top being the General Fiscal etc, Director General, Head-Merchant, Merchant, etc, as well as the descending positions and staff right down to the most lowly soldier ought, if this may so please the Honourable Gentlemen Directors, to benefit and be rewarded with a more generous salary than hitherto, in order that everybody will, all the more diligently, sincerely and honestly, serve the most lawful Company under oath and with the most humble duty and obligation. In this way, everyone should take care of his own, and nothing else but, his trusted post and duties. If something of this nature may please Your Excellency and the entire Honourable Gentlemen Directors to implement, it could be assumed, with God's blessing and assistance, to bring a good change towards improvement of usefulness and considerable progress and advantage for the most lawful Company, as well as the welfare, benefit and goodness for all of its subordinates, all of which God Himself will surely assist.

SOLI DEO GLORIA
TO THE GLORY OF GOD ALONE

POSTCRIPT

In the 21st century, many types of slavery still exist within American and European borders: men and women, young boys and girls are being sold directly into slavery for forced labour, prostitution, wide spread child pornography, child labour and other types of abuse. While many contemporary commentators acknowledge this, I continue to be amazed that Danish historians continue to ignore the slavery era in Denmark's history. Where are the schoolbooks for Danish children about these activities? More recently than this, I am often reminded that far too few Danes know about the one last tragedy of this period: that as late as 1917, sixty seven years after ceasing trading activities on the Guinea Coast, the Christian Danish State sold her West Indian islands with everything on them - men, women, children and animals - for cash, to the United States of America.

SELECTED BIBLIOGRAPHY

Balander, G. (1970) Sociology of Black Africa, Praeger Publishers, New York

Barbot, J. (1732) A Description of the Coasts of North and South Guinea, Churchill, Awnsham and John, London.

Barbot, John A. (1756) A Description of the Coasts of Guinea, I - VI, Churchills Voyages Vol. V, London.

Bosman, W., (no date) Neuwkeurige Beschryving van de Guinese Goud - Tand-enSlave-Kust, Ghana´s Archives books.

Dansk Kolonihistorie (1983) Indforing og studie, Aarhus Universitet, Aarhus.

Gemery, H. A. & Hogendorn, eds (1975) The Uncommon Market, Academic Press, New York

Green-Pedersen, Sv. E. (1974) Transactions of the Historical Society of Ghana, Vol. 15, Legon University, Accra.

Green-Pedersen, Sv. E. (1975) Transactions of the Historical Society of Ghana, Vol. 16, Legon University, Accra.

Hagen, Rune (1985) Mentalitetshistorie: Hva og Hvorfor?, Leamington, Stockholm.

Hansen, Thorkild (1987) Slavernes Kyst, Viborg, Gyldendals, Copenhagen.

Harbsmeier, M. (1987) On Travel Accounts and Cosmological Srategies, Barth, Copenhagen.

Holberg, L. (1921) Danmarks og Norges Beskrivelse, Samlede Skrifter, Vol. V., Copenhagen.

Isert, Paul E. (1788-1850) Dokumenter angaaende de af P.E. Isert Foreslaaede, Thaarups   Statistical Archives, Copenhagen.

Isert, Paul E., Reise til Guinea og de Caribaeiske Oer Samling af de Bedste og Nyeste Reisebeskrivelse, Vol. III, Copenhagen.

Jones, Adam. (1983) German Sources for West African History, Franz Steiner, Weisbaden.

Justessen, Ole (1980) Aspects of Eighteenth Century Ghanaian History, Legon University, Accra.

Kalkar, Otto, Dictionary for Old Danish Language 1300 - 1700, Copenhagen.

Kalkar, Otto, Ordbog over det danske sprog - dansk i perioden 1700 - 1950. (online dictionary of old Danish, 1700 - 1950 (ODS), Copenhagen.

Kea, Ray A. (1982) Settlements, Trade and Politics in the Seventeenth Century Gold Coast, John Hopkins University, Baltimore.

Kvium, C. (1985) Anderledshed og Historia, Stockholm.

Larsen, Kay. (1918) De Danske i Guinea, Nordiske Forfatters Forlag, Copenhagen.

Lever, J. J. (1970) Mulatto Influence in the Gold Coast in the Early Nineteenth Century, Clapp, Brooklin

Lovejoy, Paul E. (1980) The Ideology of Slavery in Africa, Toronto.

Manoukien, M. (1950) The Akan and Ga Speaking People of the Gold Coast, London.

Monrad, H.C. (1822) Bidrag til en Skildring af Guinea-Kysten og dens Indbyggere fra Aarene 1805 til 1809. København.

Meillassoux, C. (1971) The Development of Indigenous Trade and Markets in West Africa, Oxford University, Oxford.

Miers,S. & Kopytoff, J. eds. (1977) Anthropological Perspectives, Madison, UNESCO.

Phillips, Thomas. (1756) A Journal of a Voyage to Guiney and Barbados, Churchills Voyages, vol. V. 1. London.

Rask, Johannes. (1754) En Kort og Sandfærdig Rejse-Beskrivelse til og fra Guinea, Frideric Nannested, Tronhjem.

Raunklaer, I. (1917) Lægen Paul E. Iserts Breve fra Dansk Guinea. 1783-87, Købenbavn

Romer, L. F. (1756) Tilforladelig Efterretning om Negotien paa Kysten Guinea, Kiobenhavn.

Romer, L. F. (1760) Tilforladelig Efterretning om Kysten Guinea, Kiobenhavn.

Sørensen, H. E. (1992) Fridericus Africanus. Melbyhus. Skærbæk (Denmark).

Svane, F. P. A. (1748) En Kort Sandfaerdig og Omstaendelig General Declaration, (hand written) København.

Thomas, Hugh (October 1965) Slave Trade, The Observer, London.

URBAN (28 November 2006) Danish Newspaper, Copenhagen.

Vinterberg & Bodelsen, Dansk - Engelsk. 4th edition, Gyldendal, Copenhagen.

Ward, W. E. F. (1959) A History of Ghana. London.

Wilks, I. (1962) Asante in the Nineteenth Century, The Journal of African History, 3 Cabridge University, Cambridge.

Wolf, Eric. R. (1992) Europe and the People Without History, University of California.

The *Theologian* Slave Trader

ABOUT THE AUTHOR

Christiana Oware Knudsen was born and brought up in Ghana. As a young, newly trained schoolteacher, she met the Danish medical doctor, Peder Christian Kjærulff Knudsen, at Koforidua, Ghana in 1955. They married and had three children. Later on they moved to Denmark to settle. However, her family connection with Denmark goes back long before she met her husband. As this book shows, her mother's family story is interwoven in the affairs of the Danish slave-trading fortress, Christiansborg, over three hundred years ago.

Christiana Knudsen

Also, nearly two hundred years ago, Christiana Oware Knudsen's grandfather, Nana Kwaku (O)Ware, the regional chief (the Gyasehene) of the kingdom of Akyem Abuakwa, traded with the Danes for Danish guns, gunpowder and schnapps. This family trade continued with the British after Christiansborg Fortress was sold to them in 1850.

Christiana Oware Knudsen achieved her Masters degree (Cand. Phil.) in Social Anthropology from Aarhus University, Denmark. She was awarded her PhD degree in Medical Anthropology by Derby

University, United Kingdom, on the basis of research she carried out into Distant Spiritual-Healing as complementary to medical health care in the UK. She has carried out research and published books in the field of Female Circumcision (The Falling Dawadawa Tree) and Tribal Markings (The Patterned Skin) in Ghana. Recently she has published a satire about a group of Danish tourists' failure to reach their destination, Christiansborg Fortress in modern Ghana, due to their serious problems with excessive materialism. Now a pensioner, she lives in Spain where she continues to research and write.

The *Theologian* Slave Trader

www.ingramcontent.com/pod-product-compliance
Lightning Source LLC
Chambersburg PA
CBHW031313150426
43191CB00005B/208